INTRODUCTION TO PROGRAMMING IN PROLOG

Prentice Hall International
Series in Computer Science

C. A. R. Hoare, Series Editor

BACKHOUSE, R. C., *Program Construction and Verification*
BACKHOUSE, R. C., *Syntax of Programming Languages: Theory and practice*
DE BAKKER, J. W., *Mathematical Theory of Program Correctness*
BIRD, R., and WADLER, P., *Introduction to Functional Programming*
BJÖRNER, D., and JONES, C. B., *Formal Specification and Software Development*
BORNAT, R., *Programming from First Principles*
BUSTARD, D., ELDER, J., and WELSH, J., *Concurrent Program Structures*
CLARK, K. L., and MCCABE, F. G., *micro-Prolog: Programming in logic*
CROOKES, D., *Introduction to Programming in Prolog*
DROMEY, R. G., *How to Solve it by Computer*
DUNCAN, F., *Microprocessor Programming and Software Development*
ELDER, J., *Construction of Data Processing Software*
GOLDSCHLAGER, L., and LISTER, A., *Computer Science: A modern introduction (2nd edn)*
HAYES, I. (ED.), *Specification Case Studies*
HEHNER, E. C. R., *The Logic of Programming*
HENDERSON, P., *Functional Programming: Application and implementation*
HOARE, C. A. R., *Communicating Sequential Processes*
HOARE, C.A.R., and SHEPHERDSON, J. C. (EDS), *Mathematical Logic and Programming Languages*
INMOS LTD. *occam Programming Manual*
INMOS LTD. *occam 2 Reference Manual*
JACKSON, M. A., *System Development*
JOHNSTON, H., *Learning to Program*
JONES, C. B., *Systematic Software Development using VDM*
JONES, G., *Programming in occam*
JONES, G., *Programming in occam 2*
JOSEPH, M., PRASAD, V. R., and NATARAJAN, N., *A Multiprocessor Operating System*
LEW, A., *Computer Science: A mathematical introduction*
MACCALLUM, I., *Pascal for the Apple*
MACCALLUM, I., *UCSD Pascal for the IBM PC*
MEYER, B., *Object-oriented Software Construction*
PEYTON JONES, S. L., *The Implementation of Functional Programming Languages*
POMBERGER, G., *Software Engineering and Modula-2*
REYNOLDS, J. C., *The Craft of Programming*
SLOMAN, M., and KRAMER, J., *Distributed Systems and Computer Networks*
TENNENT, R. D., *Principles of Programming Languages*
WATT, D. A., WICHMANN, B. A., and FINDLAY, W., *ADA: Language and methodology*
WELSH, J., and ELDER, J., *Introduction to Modula-2*
WELSH, J., and ELDER, J., *Introduction to Pascal (3rd edn)*
WELSH, J., ELDER, J., and BUSTARD, D., *Sequential Program Structures*
WELSH, J., and HAY, A., *A Model Implementation of Standard Pascal*
WELSH, J., and MCKEAG, M., *Structured System Programming*
WIKSTRÖM, Å., *Functional Programming using Standard ML*

INTRODUCTION TO PROGRAMMING IN PROLOG

Danny Crookes

The Queen's University of Belfast,
Northern Ireland

PRENTICE HALL

NEW YORK   LONDON   TORONTO   SYDNEY   TOKYO

First published 1988 by
Prentice Hall International (UK) Ltd,
66 Wood Lane End, Hemel Hempstead,
Hertfordshire, HP2 4RG
A division of
Simon & Schuster International Group

Printed and bound in Great Britain by
A. Wheaton & Co. Ltd, Exeter.

Library of Congress Cataloging-in-Publication Data

Crookes, Danny, 1956–
  Introduction to programming in Prolog.

  Includes index.
  1. Prolog (Computer program language) I. Title.
QA76.73.P76C74 1988 005.13'3 88-4073
ISBN 0-13-710146-5

British Library Cataloguing in Publication Data

Crookes, Danny
  Introduction to programming in Prolog.
  1. Computer systems. Programming
  languages: Prolog
  I. Title
  005.13'3
  ISBN 0-13-710146-5

---

1 2 3 4 5   92 91 90 89 88

ISBN 0-13-710146-5

Contents

PART TWO   Applications of Prolog

Preface

There is a strange state of affairs which exists in the teaching of computer programming at present. It seems that beginners usually learn one of the more difficult programming languages, while it is the more experienced and advanced programmers who learn the easier programming languages. Well-established languages like BASIC and Pascal tend to be the beginner's first programming language, and these languages are far from easy for a novice to master. More recent languages like Prolog, on the other hand, are from many points of view much easier languages to learn and use than either BASIC or Pascal. Perhaps it is not surprising that things should be this way round, though. Researchers who design new languages are constantly striving to make programming languages simpler and easier to use. Their research achievements, in the form of simpler programming languages, tend to be regarded as advanced, and therefore reserved for the experienced programmer. In fact, it is the beginner who has most to gain from these advances. Sadly, it can often be the beginner who is the last to be given the opportunity to benefit. This book is a step towards rectifying this anomaly.

Using Prolog as a first programming language has much to be said for it. Even with only a very small number of programming concepts, useful programs can be written to solve many real life problems. This means that not only is the material more interesting, but by the end of a short course the learner is in a position to write programs which are useful in real life. All too often, when students in a non-computing discipline have to do some computing as part of their course, they are introduced to programming in a language such as BASIC. Even if this material is understood, the students are still a long way off being able to write useful programs for problems which they encounter in their own discipline. But with Prolog, things can be different. Whether it be only a short course of a few lectures, or perhaps a full course, all that is learnt can be immediately applied to real problems. At Queen's University Belfast, Prolog is taught to first-year students, most of whom have never used a computer before. Many continue with Computer Science, but a fair proportion will end up in other subjects such as Agriculture, or Modern Languages, or Geography, or Psychology. This book has been prepared as a result of our experience with this course. From our experience, we can certainly recommend the use of Prolog as a first programming language, either for short courses or for full-length courses. Only modesty prevents us from making a second recommendation about which text would prove most beneficial in teaching Prolog to such audiences!

For would-be computer scientists, learning Prolog in the early stages also has several advantages. Many of the more abstract concepts which are necessary in a deeper study of the subject can be introduced in a natural and understandable way using Prolog. For instance, in Chapter 6 of this book, 'An application in language translation', many key Computer Science concepts are illustrated and used: parsing, grammars, semantic checking, parse tree building, and tree-based translation. These concepts are fundamental, for instance, to an understanding of compilers. Of course, the reader is not always *told* that these are important abstract concepts, or even given all the terminology. But the seeds of the concepts are planted in an understandable way so that the foundation is there when these subjects are treated more fully at a later date.

Another group of people who could find this book useful are professional programmers who have heard much about Prolog and Expert Systems, but who have never got to grips with it all. It is no easy task to keep up to date with developments in computing, particularly when topics and trends are presented using a whole new set of jargon and buzz-words. Many of us know that uncomfortable feeling of being in a discussion on expert systems with others, while all the time not being completely sure of what an expert system actually *is*. This book should give such a reader a good grasp of the fundamentals of Prolog, and an understanding of some of its applications, including expert systems.

The material in this book can be used selectively, if necessary. Part One introduces progressively the principle features of Prolog. At each stage in the presentation — even after the second chapter — it is possible to write useful programs, even though their capacity may be limited. Part Two illustrates the use of Prolog, by considering some Prolog applications. This part has two main themes: language translation, and expert systems. The first theme is treated in Chapter 6; this is a major chapter, and introduces many of the concepts with which a computer scientist ought to be familiar. As a coverage of the issues involved in language translation *per se*, it is of course grossly simplistic; but this is unavoidable, and to a certain extent intentional. The second theme, on expert systems, is developed in three graded stages (Chapters 7, 8 and 9). First come two preparatory case studies: one from law, and one from medicine. These form the basis of the more general discussion of expert systems which comes in Chapter 9. Since the principles of expert systems are not confined purely to a Prolog context, Chapter 9 is not so much on using Prolog. Nevertheless, expert systems have proved to be a rather successful application area for Prolog. Finally comes Chapter 10, which is entitled 'Epilog'. This is not another new programming language. Rather, it takes a very brief forward look at areas beyond the coverage of this book, and asks 'What problems lie ahead if the use of Prolog is to be pursued further?' In this short chapter, the interested reader is introduced in very broad terms to problems which could be encountered, and is directed to suitable follow-up material.

This book presents a complete approach to programming which will be new to many readers. Arguably, the art of achieving success in such an ambitious venture lies more in deciding what to leave out, than in what to include! There are several features of Prolog which have deliberately not been treated in any depth in this book, for at least two reasons:

(i) A reader with only a limited amount of time to devote to learning Prolog, and who may be undertaking only a short course in the subject, will obviously want to learn those aspects of the language which will be the most useful and the most productive. This book has intentionally selected those features of Prolog which come into this category.

(ii) Some of the omitted features of Prolog actually go against the true spirit of Prolog. In many cases, they are there to improve the performance of a program which already works. There is a danger that, if these aspects are discussed in depth while learning the core of the language, then the underlying philosophy of Prolog may become obscured.

A major concern in the presentation of the material in this book has been to teach the material in as clear and as understandable a way as possible, rather than to present a definitive and formal treatise on the subject. Thus, for instance, the subject of backtracking is treated in several carefully graded stages, spread throughout the text. This is in preference to a single in-depth explanation of this difficult subject early in the text (as other books have chosen to do), which can be rather daunting to the novice.

The version of Prolog used in this book is known as Edinburgh Prolog, or DECsystem-10 Prolog. This is now more or less standard Prolog, and is substantially the same as 'core Prolog' described by Clocksin and Mellish in their book *Programming in Prolog*, published by Springer-Verlag.

Acknowledgements

The author's own interest in Prolog owes much to a year spent in the Department of Computing at Imperial College, London. Indeed, Chapter 7 includes a discussion of a project carried out by Professor Kowalski's team at Imperial College, on the British Nationality Act. Use of some of the material produced as a result of this project is gratefully acknowledged. Also, the medical diagnosis example in Chapter 8 was inspired by a delightful article by Chris Naylor called 'How to build an inferencing engine', which appeared in 'Expert Systems: Principles and case studies', edited by Richard Forsyth, and published by Chapman and Hall.

Belfast   D.C.
March, 1988

PART ONE

The language Prolog

1

Introduction

1.1 Programming for modern applications

When computers were first designed, it was never intended that they would be used anything like as widely as they are today. In fact, when one of the earliest computers was first built and demonstrated, it was reckoned that about three of the machines would be quite sufficient for Britain's needs! Computers were initially designed to be powerful calculators, to help scientists solve equations and other mathematical problems involving large amounts of rather tedious calculations. The problems which computers were employed to solve therefore tended to be well-defined, and could often be specified precisely by an equation. For instance, let us say the problem was to calculate the distance travelled by a free-falling object, such as a bomb, or a parachutist. A mathematician can supply us with a formula to calculate this distance. Say we want to know the distance travelled in a given length of time T, starting from some initial downward speed I. Ignoring wind resistance, the equation which defines the distance travelled by the falling object (in metres) is:

$$distance = I\,T + \tfrac{1}{2} g\, T^2$$

In this formula, g stands for gravity, and is approximately 9.81. It is not necessary to understand this formula to be able to use it. Given actual values for the initial speed I, and the time T, it is not difficult to plug these values into the formula, do a series of calculations, and produce a result. For instance, if I is zero and T is ten, the distance travelled is:

$$distance = 490.5\ metres$$

Setting out the required individual calculations in more detail gives a sequence of steps which anyone could follow, perhaps with the help of a

3

calculator. If we try to be completely precise, so as not to leave anything open to doubt, we might come up with the following sequence of steps for the complete calculation:

> { calculate the first term }
> *multiply I by T; call the result A, say;*

> { calculate the second term }
> *multiply T by T; call the result B;*
> *multiply B by g; call the result C;*
> *divide C by 2; call the result D;*

> { add both terms }
> *add A and D   ; call the result distance*

This sequence of steps is in fact the basis of a computer program to do the calculation. This list would be followed step by step by the computer, though rather more quickly than we ourselves could manage. The process of breaking any task down into a sequence of steps like this is the essence of the traditional approach to computer programming.

To make the task of writing programs like this more convenient, better programming languages were designed. One particularly well-known language is FORTRAN. The term FORTRAN stands for FORMula TRANslation. In FORTRAN, a programmer would merely have to write:

```
DISTANCE = I * T + G * T * T / 2
```

where '*' stands for multiplication and '/' stands for division. Even though it first appeared back in 1957, FORTRAN is still very useful for scientific and mathematical problems, where the problem can be specified precisely.

At the same time as it was becoming clear how successful computers could be in scientific applications, people were wondering if computers could be just as successful in other areas. One obvious candidate for computerisation was commercial data processing. Large amounts of time, money and effort were being spent in the commercial world on manual tasks like wage calculations, pay-rolls, and other boring but necessary data processing. The potential savings which computerisation offered, plus the additional services and facilities which could in theory be provided by using a computer, proved too tempting to resist. Thus the whole area of commercial data processing became another application area for computers. Programmers who worked in this area developed programming languages which were more suited to data processing than to scientific computing. One particularly successful data processing language was COBOL. Data processing languages like COBOL reflected the shift away from doing large amounts of calculation, to an emphasis on storing and using large amounts of information.

More recently, however, the computer industry has become a victim of its own success. As people's expectations grew, and as the cost of the actual equipment fell, the number of application areas for computers mushroomed. Instead of sticking to applications which seemed obviously suited to computers (machine-oriented applications), more and more attempts have been made to have computers take over tasks which come more naturally to humans (human-oriented applications). Some examples of these application areas are:

- medical diagnosis
- oil exploration
- management advisers
- language translation
- human speech recognition
- many, many others

One feature of human-oriented applications like these is that the computer has to process what we might call *knowledge*, rather than just data consisting of facts and figures. So instead of storing the medical records of patients as bare facts, a modern medical computing system might be expected to store and use general knowledge in the form of *rules*, such as:

> *Someone who has a sore throat and a headache*
> *could have influenza*

The human brain is very good at processing knowledge. But as programmers began to undertake the task of programming these more modern applications, it soon became apparent that computers were not at all geared to working with knowledge, rather than just factual information. The experience in the programming industry over the last twenty years or so has been somewhat bitter in this regard; in particular, two major problems have been identified:

(i) It can be very difficult to specify precisely what the problem *is*, never mind how to solve it.
(ii) Actually writing the programs, or *software*, has proved extremely slow, expensive and error-prone. For problems which involve using knowledge, it seems that our mental concept of how *we* would solve the problem does not fit naturally into the more traditional step-by-step programming approach. Thus there is a disparity between the way humans usually work things out, and the way computers have traditionally worked things out.

In the early 1970s, the computing industry woke up to the difficulty of producing software. It became apparent that the software was actually more expensive and less reliable than the actual computer equipment, or *hardware*. It was also obvious that the problem was getting worse as time went on. This state of affairs became known as the *Software Crisis*, and it forced a major rethink of how programs should be written. Many different avenues were investigated. Attempts were made to develop techniques for defining problems very precisely. Previously unfashionable ways of thinking about programming were explored, and new ways were invented. Many of these involved going back to ideas in mathematics. Some turned out to be unproductive, but others have opened up new approaches to programming. One of the most successful new programming approaches, for problems which involve storing and using knowledge of one sort or another, is called *logic programming*. It is the one for which the language Prolog has been designed. Let us now look at the basis of this approach.

1.2   A new way of programming

Traditionally, computers have been programmed to work things out using a step-by-step approach, such as: '*do this; do that; do the other; then do it all again ten times*'. But this is not really how humans typically work things out. So perhaps we should ask: how *do* humans work things out? For many everyday problems, the answer is:

> *by logical reasoning*

For instance, suppose you are given the statements:

> *All rich men are chauvinists*
> *Fred is a man*
> *Fred is rich*

The first of these is a general rule; the second two statements are just facts. You are then asked the question:

> *Is Fred a chauvinist?*

Almost without thinking, you can work out logically that the answer is:

> *Yes*

Take another example; suppose you are given the statements:

> *Janet likes anyone who is rich*
> *Programmers are rich if they use Prolog*
> *John is bald*
> *Janet uses COBOL*
> *John uses Prolog*
> *John is a programmer*

Here, we have two general rules, and four facts. This time, the question is:

> *Does Janet like John?*

From the given rules and facts, we can infer logically that the answer is again:

Yes

Now try to analyse the thought processes in answering the two questions so far, and follow the argument in slow motion. In the first case, we had to prove the theory that:

Fred is a chauvinist

How was this done? There were several steps in this logical argument:

(i) Although there is no statement which specifically states that Fred is a chauvinist, we do have a rule which states that someone is a chauvinist if the person is both rich, and a man. So we have reduced the problem to having to prove firstly that Fred is rich, and secondly, that he is a man. We now proceed to prove these two theories separately. They are both simpler than the original theory.

(ii) Is Fred rich? The third statement states that Fred is indeed rich.

(iii) Is Fred a man? The second statement likewise states that Fred is a man.

The logical conclusion is therefore that Fred is indeed a chauvinist.

The second example is slightly more involved, but follows the same pattern. We are aiming to prove that:

Janet likes John

The logical steps in this argument are as follows:

(i) Although we are not told specifically that Janet likes John, we do have a rule about who Janet likes. So does John come into this category? The first statement implies that Janet likes John provided John is rich. So we now only have to prove that John is rich, and we will then have proved that Janet likes John.

(ii) Is John rich? Again, since this is not explicitly stated, we look for a statement which defines who is rich, and see if John is one of these people. The second statement implies that John is rich if John is a programmer, and if he uses Prolog. These two conditions have now to be considered separately; if both turn out to be true, we will have proved that John is indeed rich.

(iii) Is John a programmer? The very last statement proves this, by definition.

(iv) Does John use Prolog? The last statement but one confirms this, by definition.

Therefore, by logical deduction, we know that Janet likes John. So we can answer Yes to the original question.

Perhaps by now there seems something fairly methodical, even mechanical, about the logical reasoning process which we have used to answer a question, given certain rules and facts. It is rather like being an unimaginative but thorough detective. Given a conjecture which has to be verified, or a 'theory' which has to be either proved or disproved, we might make an attempt at describing the general strategy as follows:

(i) Is there a fact which states immediately that the theory is true? If so, we need go no further. If not, then:

(ii) Is there a more general rule which would guarantee the theory to be correct *under certain conditions?* If not, we have failed to prove it. But if so, then the problem has been reduced to proving each of these conditions individually. These should be considered as mini-theories in their own right, and this same overall reasoning process should be applied to each one in turn, starting from (i) above. If *all* the conditions can be proved, then the original theory has been proved.

Given a set of statements which define what is known about a particular problem, and a question which has to be answered on the basis of that knowledge, we as humans seem able to follow through this logical reasoning process quite naturally. But it is a rather different process to the step-by-step '*do this; then do that*' process which computers traditionally follow. The task of using a computer in a more human-oriented application would be rather easier if the computer was itself able to reason logically. So the $64,000 question is:

> *Can computers be made to follow this*
> *mechanical process of logical reasoning?*

The answer is 'Yes', and it has already been done. One language which has this simple built-in logical reasoning ability is Prolog. Prolog stands for **Pro**gramming in **log**ic. It is this language, and the approach to programming which Prolog was designed to support, which is the subject of this book.

Perhaps a word of caution might be in order, though. A simple logical reasoning ability such as we have described is not necessarily the same as human intelligence. Human thinking may well be more than just this fairly simple approach to logical reasoning. The issue of whether or not intelligence is the result of logical reasoning alone is a distinctly thorny philosophical question, which we will not attempt to tackle.

1.3   A closer look at applications

At the heart of most commercial applications is a stored base of information, usually called a *database*. Also, many of the more recent systems of this type are *interactive*, in that the user interacts with the system on a question and answer basis. Answering a question from a user involves processing in some way the data held in the database. Sometimes this processing will be very simple, perhaps even just looking it up. But in more sophisticated systems it might be very complex. The general structure of this type of system is:

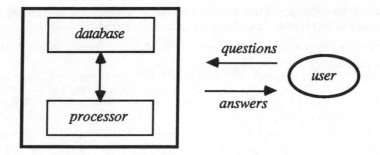

Depending on the complexity of the processing which takes place when answering a question, we can classify many applications (including the emerging modern ones) into the following four categories. We will present them in increasing order of sophistication.

Database systems

The information component at the heart of a database system is just a collection of facts. There may be only a few facts, or there may be millions; but it is still just a collection of specific facts.

The processing component of a database system merely provides a lookup facility, where information already in the database can be retrieved in response to a question from the user. There will also be a facility for adding new facts to the database during its lifetime.

If we take an application from the field of medicine, say, then an example of this type of system might be a medical records system. The database would perhaps contain a list of relevant medical facts about each person in the system, such as:

> *date of birth*
> *blood group*
> *history of check-ups*
> *details of any previous illnesses*

Given a database of information like this, the processing component could work out answers to questions such as:

> *What is Mrs Robinson's blood group?*

and

> *Who has had measles?*

These can be answered by looking up the stored facts, even if it requires a laborious search through the whole database.

This type of system is undoubtedly very useful, but it does have its limitations when it comes to the type of question which it can answer. For instance, it would be unable to handle a query such as:

> *Is Mr Jones likely to have a heart attack?*

Unless the database explicitly states for each individual whether or not they are likely to have a heart attack, the answer to this question would have to be worked out on the basis of some more general medical principles, rather than just specific facts. Because this requires more than a simple lookup facility, this type of question cannot be handled by a straightforward database system.

Intelligent databases

An intelligent database goes beyond the previous type of database system, in that it has the ability to hold and to follow *general rules*, as well as specific facts. The database component of an intelligent database thus has two parts: specific facts, and general rules.

To be able to apply general rules to answer specific questions, the processing component must have a certain ability to carry out logical reasoning, of the type discussed previously in section 1.2. To answer a specific question, the processing component will first see if the necessary information is stored as an explicit fact; if not, it will have to try to work it out, by applying the general rules which it has available.

In our medical records example, an intelligent database would have the capability to answer a question such as:

> *On the basis of blood groups, could Johnny*
> *possibly be a child of Mr and Mrs Smith?*

There are well-defined medical rules about blood groups which, if followed, lead to a definite yes/no answer to this question. The database component in this case would need to contain specific facts about the blood groups of the three people involved, and also the medical rules about blood group relationships.

Thus an intelligent database can infer new facts dynamically, rather than having to store absolutely every piece of specific information it is likely to need. So, given suitable facts and rules, this type of system could answer the query:

> *Is Mr Jones likely to have a heart attack?*

However, the answer would only be either yes or no, and this would give us no indication of whether there is, say, a one in a thousand chance as opposed to a one in ten chance. An intelligent database, therefore, cannot handle questions such as:

How likely is it that Mr Jones will have a heart attack?

This problem comes into the next category of application.

Expert systems

Many real systems are so complex that there may be no single definite answer to a question. Instead, there may be several possible answers, each with a different measure of certainty, or probability. For instance, given facts stating that a patient has the symptoms:

> *headache*
> *stiff neck*
> *sore back*

consider the question:

> *From what is the patient likely to be suffering?*

Based on experience and a knowledge of medical matters, the answer might be the following set of possibilities:

> *influenza*   *(probability 0.75)*
> *hangover*   *(probability 0.15)*
> *meningitis*   *(probability 0.05)*
> *other unknown causes* *(probability 0.05)*

In the real world, situations like this usually require the services of a specialist or *expert*, who makes value judgements based on experience and specialised knowledge. Computerising this process, and storing an expert's knowledge of the subject as the database component, gives what is known as an *Expert System*. The general structure of an expert system can be viewed as shown below in Figure 1.1; this also shows the terminology which tends to be used for an expert system.

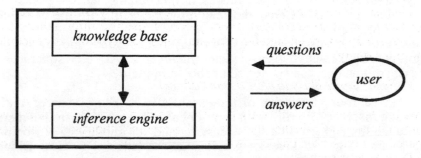

Figure 1.1 *Structure of an expert system*

In an expert system, the database component represents the system's knowledge of the subject. It includes specific facts and general rules, but these will also have to contain some sort of statistical information, perhaps specifying how likely it is that each fact or rule will apply. The processor component not only draws inferences, but must be able to follow several different trains of reasoning, and cope with the varying degrees of certainty which each has.

Learning systems

In an expert system, the knowledge base contains statistical information; in a medical application, this might include information on how common each possible illness is. All this statistical information must be supplied by whoever builds the system; the inference engine thereafter slavishly sticks to whatever information it is given, and does not modify its basic behaviour in the light of experience. This is rather different from what happens when humans carry out the same task. In practice, a human's knowledge base grows with experience; indeed, this is often how much of the knowledge base is built up in the first place. An expert system relies on being told this information, rather than working it out itself.

A computerised system which mimics this human process of *learning* could therefore start off with a relatively small knowledge base, and build up its specialist knowledge over a period of time. For instance, it could work out that, say, influenza is rather more common than meningitis by noticing that it encounters more cases of one than of the other. To do this, it must have some inbuilt *observer* as part of its processor component, which looks out for patterns and trends, and modifies the knowledge base in the light of experience. Again, after a period of time, a system with this degree of sophistication might even be able to notice a connection between, say, smoking and incidences of heart attacks, without being told. So if we asked the question:

Is Mr Jones likely to have a heart attack?

the answer to this question would be arrived at as the result of having observed previous cases of heart attacks, noting common characteristics of the victims' personal details, and matching these up with the personal details of Mr Jones.

Systems like this are obviously rather sophisticated, and are in the realms of what is referred to as *Artificial Intelligence* (AI). The structure of a system of this type can be viewed as shown in Figure 1.2.

Thus, these four categories differ essentially in the power of their reasoning machine, or processing component. This can vary from a mere lookup facility right up to a self-observing and self-modifying reasoning mechanism. The last three categories span the range of systems which have become known as:

Intelligent Knowledge Based Systems

or IKBS for short.

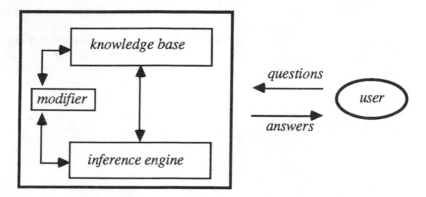

Figure 1.2 *Structure of a learning system*

1.4   Conclusion

The programming language Prolog has all the built-in mechanisms for directly constructing database systems and intelligent databases (the first and second of the four categories above). In both these cases, the processing component, or reasoning mechanism, is a standard part of the Prolog system. This system has a powerful lookup facility, and a fairly straightforward logical reasoning ability. However, this mechanism is not powerful enough for the inference engine of expert systems and learning systems (the third and fourth of the above categories). Once it becomes necessary to introduce some degree of uncertainty, the inference engine section must be written by the programmer. This can of course be done using Prolog, as we shall see. In either of these cases, however, Prolog is a very suitable notation for representing the knowledge base.

Prolog itself began life quietly in Marseilles and at Imperial College, London, in the early 1970s. Perhaps surprisingly, it didn't attract much attention at first, and wasn't viewed as a serious contender for the world's favourite programming language. However, the situation changed dramatically later in the 1970s, with the announcement by the Japanese of their Fifth Generation Computer Project. The Japanese argued that future computer systems would need to be able to process *knowledge* rather than just data. They decided to standardise their programming for this on the language Prolog, which was one of the few languages around at the time which provided a means of representing knowledge. The future of Prolog was assured overnight. Many other countries responded to the Japanese initiative by setting up their own national research programmes, so as not to be left behind.

One result of the Japanese initiative, and the other research programmes which it prompted, is that Prolog has somehow become associated with Artificial Intelligence and other rather difficult and advanced topics. This has given the impression that it is a language for experts only, and not for novices. This is unfortunate, because in many respects Prolog is a much more suitable language for less experienced programmers than many more popular languages, such as BASIC or Pascal. This book is intended as a contribution to the effort to convey this message to the programming world.

2

Representing facts in Prolog

A Prolog statement *describes* something, or a state of affairs, rather than giving a command to do something. It is a statement of a fact which is timeless. In the simple form of Prolog statement which we introduce in this chapter, a statement is unconditional: it states that something is true, all the time, and under all circumstances. Let us start with some simple examples.

2.1   Stating simple facts

Suppose we want to describe relationships between people in a group, in which one of the people, Fred, has set his heart on another person in the group, Elizabeth. The fact that Fred likes Elizabeth would be written in Prolog as:

```
likes (fred, elizabeth).
```

In general, something which we would say in English as:

subject verb object

is written in Prolog as:

verb (*subject, object*)

or, more generally, as:

relationship (*object1, object2*)

In the one Prolog fact which we have so far, `likes` is the relationship, and `fred` and `elizabeth` are both objects. A relationship is sometimes called a *predicate* in Prolog, and the objects which are related are called *arguments* or *parameters*. A statement of a fact in Prolog is called a *clause*.

As another example, suppose we wish to state which make of car various people drive. In a statement such as:

>*Michael drives a Jaguar*

the verb or relationship is *drives*. In Prolog terminology, the predicate name is `drives`, and the arguments are the objects `michael` and `jaguar`. This gives the following Prolog clause which expresses the above fact:

```
drives (michael, jaguar).
```

Note that there can be several clauses for the same predicate. Thus, for instance, we could define the following clauses, which also state who drives what:

```
drives (elizabeth, aston_martin).
drives (fred, massey_ferguson).
```

These state that Elizabeth drives an Aston Martin, while Fred has a more agricultural means of transport.

Some details about defining facts

When actually typing Prolog facts into the computer, it is important to note the following details:

- The names of predicates and objects must begin with a lower-case letter rather than with a capital letter. Thus you should type `fred` and not `Fred`.
- A fact must be terminated with a full stop.
- Note that the underscore character '_' can be used in the middle of a name to make the name more readable.

Defining properties

Not all facts in English are relationships between two objects. Sometimes we wish to make statements such as:

>*Elizabeth is rich*

or

>*Joe is intelligent*

which do not have the standard '*subject—verb—object*' structure. But this is not a problem in Prolog, because a predicate can have any number of arguments, even just one. Thus these facts can be expressed as:

```
rich (elizabeth).
intelligent (joe).
```

These are examples of facts which state that a particular object has a certain *property*. The property acts as the relationship. The general structure of statements like this is:

property (*object*)

Numbers as objects

An object can be a *name* which we are free to make up ourselves. Examples which we have already met are `jaguar` or `elizabeth`. Alternatively, objects can also be *numbers* (whole numbers, called integers). Relationships including numbers are defined like any other relationship. For instance, the age of a person can be defined as a simple fact; if Fred is 37 years old, while Mary happens to be a youthful 19, then this information can be defined by two Prolog clauses:

```
age (fred, 37).
age (mary, 19).
```

Or, the price of items in a store could be defined in a similar way. If a radio costs $19 and a TV costs $350, this would be stated in Prolog as:

```
price (radio, 19).
price (tv, 350).
```

Symmetric relationships

In our very first example, note that the fact that Fred likes Elizabeth in no way implies that Elizabeth likes Fred. This lack of symmetry is a feature of Prolog as well as of real life. Thus in general, the Prolog statement:

relationship (*object1, object2*)

is quite different from, and does not imply:

relationship (*object2, object1*)

If the relationship we are defining is in fact symmetrical, in Prolog we have to define both aspects, as two separate facts. For instance, to state that Jeff and Pam are married to each other would require two clauses in Prolog:

```
married_to (jeff, pam).
married_to (pam, jeff).
```

We know that one must imply the other, but Prolog does not, since it has no idea of what the relationship married_to means. In fact, Prolog does not understand the meaning of *any* predicate names or objects which the programmer makes up. So it would not object to the clause:

```
fly (pigs).
```

or even to meaningless clauses like:

```
nargle (bargle, fargle).
```

A Prolog program for an employment agency

Imagine an employment agency which holds on the one hand a collection of job vacancies, and on the other hand a set of trained people looking for employment. The fact that an employer has a vacancy for someone with a particular skill or training can be defined in Prolog by a predicate:

```
has_vacancy (employer, skill)
```

For instance, the fact that NASA has a vacancy for a programmer is defined in Prolog as:

```
has_vacancy (nasa, programmer).
```

Also, the fact that a person looking for a job has been trained in a particular skill can be defined by a Prolog predicate:

```
trained_as (person, skill)
```

So the fact that Elizabeth has been trained as a secretary is defined in Prolog as:

```
trained_as (elizabeth, secretary).
```

Now suppose that our employment agency has a set of vacancies and potential trained employees; these can now be defined by the following set of Prolog facts:

```
has_vacancy (harvard, secretary).
has_vacancy (prentice_hall, author).
has_vacancy (ibm, salesman).
has_vacancy (hertz, driver).
has_vacancy (nasa, programmer).
```

```
has_vacancy (prentice_hall, secretary).

trained_as (elizabeth, secretary).
trained_as (michael, salesman).
trained_as (michael, programmer).
trained_as (joe, driver).
trained_as (mary, secretary).
trained_as (fred, taxidermist).
```

This is in fact a Prolog program, and we will be referring to it throughout this chapter. It is just a small database. On its own, it is not a command to *do* anything: it merely states facts and describes things. It has to be typed into the computer so that it can be used later on. The manual of the particular Prolog system you are using will explain how to do this. The exact details of this tend to vary from one Prolog system to another and are not, strictly speaking, part of the language itself.

We do not usually speak of *running* a program like this, as might be the case with other programming languages. Instead, we ask questions, called *queries*. When the Prolog system receives a query, it consults the facts in the program, using logical reasoning to answer the query, and displays its answers on the screen. The Prolog system corresponds to the simple logical reasoning mechanism of an intelligent database, which was mentioned in Chapter 1. It is sometimes referred to as the *system*, or even just *Prolog*.

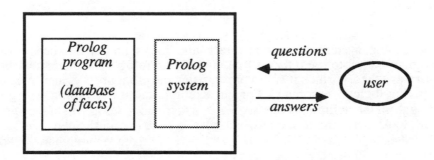

There are different types of query, depending on what sort of answer we require.

2.2   Questions with a yes/no answer

When we have a question which can be phrased in the terms:

Is it true that ... ?

we really have a *theory* which we would like either verified or disproved by the computer, on the basis of the facts in the program. For instance, in English we might wish to ask:

Is it true that Elizabeth is trained as a secretary?

Expressed in Prolog, our theory is that:

```
trained_as (elizabeth, secretary).
```

To put this theory, called a *query*, to the Prolog system, we merely enter it whenever the system is ready to receive the next query. The system indicates this by displaying the system 'prompt'. Again, the exact form of this prompt will vary depending on the version of Prolog in use; we will use:

```
?-
```

Whenever this prompt appears, it means that the system is ready and waiting to receive our next query. So our query about Elizabeth would appear as:

```
?-trained_as (elizabeth, secretary).
```

The general form of this type of query is:

```
?- fact.
```

The Prolog system takes this query and looks up its database (the program), to try to see if *fact* is true. In effect, Prolog takes the fact in the query as a theory which it has to prove, using the program as evidence, and applying logical reasoning. For our example question, Prolog will go through all the definitions of `trained_as`, in the order in which they are held, looking for the first one which matches the one in the question. In our example, the first definition of `trained_as` matches straightaway, so the system will display the answer:

```
yes
```

Thus a user who was unable to examine the actual program would now know that Elizabeth is trained as a secretary. If the user now wanted to know if Fred is trained as a secretary, then the question the user should ask is:

```
?-trained_as (fred, secretary).
```

Given the facts about `trained_as` in the program above, the system would not be able to prove this to be the case, and would display:

no

This does not mean that the program contained positive evidence that Fred has had *no* secretarial training. A no answer merely indicates that the theory could not be proved from the given facts in the program. There were no facts in the program which matched the one supplied in the query. Anything which the program does not state to be true is assumed to be false.

Here are some more examples to give practice in formulating simple queries. We assume that all the example facts given to date have been input and are part of the program.

(i) *Does Michael drive a Jaguar?* In Prolog:

```
?-drives (michael, jaguar).
```

(ii) *Does IBM have a vacancy for a programmer?* In Prolog:

```
?-has_vacancy (ibm, programmer).
```

(iii) *Is Mary rich?* In Prolog:

```
?-rich (mary).
```

(iv) *Is Fred really 37?* In Prolog:

```
?-age (fred, 37).
```

Compound queries

The form of the query can be more complex than just seeking verification of a simple fact. We can ask compound queries of the form:

Is it true that ... and ... and ... ?

In Prolog, this query is phrased using a comma for 'and'; sometimes the 'and' operation is referred to as *conjunction*:

```
?- fact1, fact2, ...
```

For instance, suppose our employment agent wishes to know if Mary has any chance of getting a job with IBM as a secretary. The query the agent should ask is:

```
?-trained_as (mary, secretary),
   has_vacancy (ibm, secretary).
```

This query consists of two parts, sometimes called *subgoals*, and the overall theory to be proved is then called the *goal*. For the goal to be true, or to *succeed*, both subgoals must succeed. The system would attempt to prove this goal in two stages. The first subgoal:

```
trained_as (mary, secretary)
```

would be considered first. Once this is proved (as it will be), the second subgoal is attempted. Given the facts in our program, this second subgoal will fail, since IBM are not recorded as having any vacancies for secretaries. Thus, the overall attempt to prove this compound query will fail, and the system will display the answer:

```
no
```

If the question had been asked the other way round:

```
?-has_vacancy (ibm, secretary),
   trained_as (mary, secretary).
```

then the answer will obviously be the same; however, the train of reasoning will be slightly different. The system will again begin by taking the first subgoal, which in this case is:

```
has_vacancy (ibm, secretary)
```

and will find that this fails. There is now no need to consider the second subgoal at all, since it cannot alter the overall result. So Prolog will return the answer no immediately upon failing at the first stage.

We can have as many conditions as we like in a query. For instance, the question:

Is Fred a rich programmer who drives an Aston Martin?

could be reformulated as:

Is Fred rich, and
is Fred a programmer, and
does Fred drive an Aston Martin?

This would then be expressed in Prolog as the query:

```
?-rich (fred),
   programmer (fred),
   drives (fred, aston_martin).
```

More general queries

All the queries so far have been very specific, involving facts about named objects. In answering a query, the Prolog system has looked for an exact match of the supplied goal. Often, though, we need a bit more flexibility. Suppose, for instance, that our employment agent is still trying to get Mary a job as a secretary. Having not had any luck with IBM, the agent would now like to ask:

Does any employer have a vacancy for a secretary?

If a query can include only specific, named employers, then this question has to be presented as a series of queries:

Does Harvard have a vacancy for a secretary?
Does Prentice Hall have a vacancy for a secretary?
...

for every employer in the database. There are two reasons why this is not a very good idea:

(i) For a large database, the whole process becomes very tedious.
(ii) What if the agent does not actually *know* the names of all the employers in the database?

The agent's question could be expressed in Prolog if we could present a query such as:

```
?-has_vacancy (does not matter who occupies this position,
                secretary).
```

To indicate that the first position in the relationship has_vacancy does not matter to us, Prolog allows us to use a special object:

```
?-has_vacancy (_, secretary).
```

The special token '_' stands for 'anything', and is called in Prolog an *anonymous variable*. It is a *variable* because it is free to take on any value which would lead to successful matching of the query with the facts in the program. It will match with *any* object. It is *anonymous* because it does not have a name. We will see soon that Prolog variables usually do have names.

In answering this query, the Prolog system will attempt to match the given 'fact':

```
has_vacancy (_, secretary).
```

w... the facts in the program in turn. Any fact which does not have secretary as the second object will not match. However, the anonymous variable will match any object. If a match is found, then the system will display the usual answer:

```
yes
```

If no match is found, the answer no will be displayed. Thus, asking a query which contains the anonymous variable is really asking:

Can a value be given to the anonymous variable such that ... ?

Given our earlier question:

```
?-has_vacancy (_, secretary).
```

the system will go through each fact in the program in turn, starting from the top, until a matching fact is encountered. A matching fact is one which has anything in the first position, and secretary in the second. In this case, the query is satisfied by the fact:

```
has_vacancy (harvard, secretary).
```

so the answer yes is returned. If no matching fact had been found (because no definition of has_vacancy has secretary in the second position), then the system would have returned the answer no.

A few more example queries might help to consolidate the ground covered so far. We give first the English formulation of the query, and then how it would be expressed in Prolog:

(i) *Does NASA have any vacancies?* In Prolog, this would be:

```
?-has_vacancy (nasa, _).
```

(ii) *Does anyone have a vacancy for a driver?* In Prolog:

```
?-has_vacancy (_, driver).
```

(iii) *Do Fred and Joe both drive a Porsche?* In Prolog:

```
?-drives (fred, porsche),
   drives (joe, porsche).
```

(iv) *Are Elizabeth and Mary both trained as secretaries?* In Prolog:

```
?-trained_as (elizabeth, secretary),
   trained_as (mary, secretary).
```

2.3   Getting more than a yes/no answer

Usually when we ask a question, we would like more than a straight 'Yes' or 'No' answer. Imagine stopping someone and asking them *'Do you have the time?'*. They pause, look at their watch, answer *'Yes'*, and walk on. That is where we end up by using only the facilities we have at present. For instance, if our agent asked the question in Prolog:

```
?-has_vacancy (_, secretary).
```

and received a positive answer, then the agent would quite like to know who it is who has the vacancy. But because the variable supplied in this query is anonymous, we cannot get at this information. What the agent would really like to ask is:

> *Is there an employer who has a vacancy for a secretary, and if so, who is it?*

This query can be presented using a new feature of Prolog, as:

```
?-has_vacancy (Employer, secretary).
```

Note: In this query, Employer is actually another *variable*, except this time it has a name, unlike the anonymous variable. The Prolog system knows that Employer is a variable rather than an object because its name begins with a capital letter.

Initially, the variable Employer is free to take on any value which would bring about a successful match, just like the anonymous variable. However, once it has been matched with something in the first position of a matching has_vacancy fact, it is from that moment set, or *bound*, to that value; it will not match any other thereafter. Think of the matching process as taking a goal and a program statement, and *trying* to make them equal. To achieve this, the Prolog system can give whatever value is necessary to free variables, but cannot change the value of set, or *bound*, variables. In Prolog terminology, this matching process is called *unification*.

When the Prolog system finds a solution to a query, it will print out the values given to variables used in the query. This is how we get specific answers back. Only if the query contains no variables does the system respond just with the simple answer yes. Thus, given our earlier set of facts defining the relationship has_vacancy, the Prolog system would respond to the above query with the answer:

```
Employer = harvard
```

It worked this out by going through the facts for has_vacancy in the program, trying to match each in turn with the query. Remember that a variable which has not yet been bound to a specific object will match with any object. The first fact succeeds, binding `Employer` to `harvard`, and displaying the value given to the variable `Employer`.

At this point, the system will pause, and wait for further instructions from the user. The reason it waits is that the user may either be satisfied with this *single* answer or may, on the other hand, want to know if there are any more answers to the query (i.e. if there are any more employers who have a vacancy for a secretary). If no more answers are required, the user at this point merely hits the *Return* key on the keyboard. However, if the user is interested in more answers, the user indicates this by typing a semicolon before hitting the *Return* key. This will cause the system to carry on *from where it left off*, continuing the matching process.

So if we wished to discover all those who have vacancies for a secretary, we would keep asking for more answers. This would be done by typing semicolon after each new set of answers, until the answer `no` finally came up. This would result in the following interaction:

```
?-has_vacancy (Employer, secretary).

Employer = harvard;
Employer = prentice_hall;
no
```

Note the need to be careful about beginning object names with a lower-case letter, and variables with an upper-case letter. This is a common source of error when defining Prolog facts or submitting queries. For instance, if by mistake we entered the query:

```
?-trained_as (fred, Secretary).
```

the system would respond with the rather confusing answer:

```
Secretary = taxidermist
```

because it has interpreted `Secretary` as a variable and not as an object.

Using variables to look up information stored in the program is fairly straightforward, as the following examples show. The answers given in each case assume that the definitions of the predicates in question which have been presented earlier in this chapter have been added to the program.

(i) *What age is Mary?* In Prolog:

```
?-age (mary, A).
```

This gives the answer:

```
A = 19
```

(ii) *What price is a radio?* In Prolog:

```
?-price (radio, P).

P = 19
```

(iii) *Who drives which sort of car?* Here, both arguments are variables:

```
?-drives (Driver, Make).
```

Based on the three earlier facts about drives, the answer would be:

```
Driver = michael
Make = jaguar;
Driver = elizabeth
Make = aston_martin;
Driver = fred
Make = massey_ferguson;
no
```

Using variables in compound queries

The use of variables in a query can be particularly helpful when the query is compound. A compound query is one with several parts or subgoals, all of which must be true for the query to succeed. For instance, if our agent wishes to know if there is an employer who has a vacancy for someone with Elizabeth's skills, then this query would be phrased as:

```
?-has_vacancy (Employer, Skill),
   trained_as (elizabeth, Skill).
```

This is read as: is there an employer (called Employer) who has a vacancy for someone with a particular skill (called Skill), and has Elizabeth been trained in this skill? This would produce the response:

```
Employer = harvard
Skill = secretary;
Employer = prentice_hall
Skill = secretary
```

Note: The use of the same variable name (Skill) in both subgoals means that the skill in each case must be the same. This is a general rule in Prolog: the use of the same variable name at two different places within a query means that the objects which eventually occupy those positions must be the same object.

As another example, suppose we wanted to know if Joe and Michael drive the same sort of car. This would be expressed in Prolog as:

```
?-drives (joe, Car), drives (michael, Car).
```

As it happens, if the program contains only the definitions of `drives`
given at the start of this chapter, Michael and Joe do not drive the same sort
of car; so the system would respond just with a `no` answer.

Let us take a few more example queries. We assume that in each case
all possible answers to the query are wanted; so the system will return as
many different substitutions for the variables as it can find. These
examples are also used to raise some other issues, so they will not be
completely straightforward.

(i) *Are there any matches of vacancies with potential employees?* In
Prolog, this would be phrased as:

```
?-has_vacancy (Employer, Skill),
   trained_as (Person, Skill).
```

and would produce the answers beginning with:

```
Employer = harvard
Skill = secretary
Person = elizabeth;
Employer = harvard
Skill = secretary
Person = mary;
Employer = ibm
Skill = salesman
Person = michael;
...
```

(ii) *What competition does Mary have in looking for a job?* We might
define a competitor of Mary as someone who has been trained in a skill
in which Mary has also been trained. Phrasing this in Prolog gives:

```
?-trained_as (mary, Skill),
   trained_as (Competitor, Skill).
```

Given our existing program defining how each person has been
trained, this would produce the answer:

```
Skill = secretary
Competitor = elizabeth;
Skill = secretary
Competitor = mary;
no
```

The strange thing is that Mary comes out as one of her own
competitors! How has this come about? Substituting `mary` for

`Competitor` in the query certainly causes the query to be satisfied. The fact is, we have not been as precise in our definition of a competitor as we should have been. Strictly speaking, a competitor of Mary is someone *else* who has been trained in the same skill as Mary, where by *else* we mean someone who is not Mary. Thus we need a third condition, stating that `Competitor` is not `mary`. Saying that something is *not* the case in Prolog can be a thorny philosophical problem, since Prolog facts state what is true rather than what is false. Leaving this issue aside, however, in Prolog we state that something is not the case by writing the condition:

    not *(fact)*

This succeeds if *fact* fails, and fails if *fact* succeeds. So to express the third condition above, that `Competitor` is not `mary`, we would write:

    not (Competitor = mary)

The entire query then becomes:

    ?-trained_as (mary, Skill),
       trained_as (Competitor, Skill),
       not (Competitor = mary).

A word of warning about using '='. Testing if two objects are equal involves testing if they are the *same object*. This is not as straightforward as it seems; for instance, what is the effect of testing if an object is equal to a variable which is still free, and has not yet got a value? Thus, '=' in Prolog is defined rather differently, in such a way that:

`mary = mary`	is *true*;
`mary = elizabeth`	is *false*;
`mary = X`	is *true* if X is `mary`;
	false if X has any other value;
	true if X is free
	(and X will be set to `mary` in the process)

Think of '=' as trying to make its two sides equal. It is actually the same as the usual Prolog matching process of unification.

Finding answers in order

When all possible answers to a query are asked for, the answers can sometimes be a little surprising. Perhaps some of the answers above surprised you at first sight. Understanding why the system responds the way it does requires some knowledge of the internal operation of the Prolog system and its logical reasoning process; this will be dealt with in more detail in Chapter 3, but some information is given here to explain a few of the effects which can arise.

Finding all possible answers is a bit like finding all combinations. For instance, suppose you were asked to list all the combinations of the two letters A and B, allowing duplications. There are four in all:

```
A  A
A  B
B  A
B  B
```

When these are listed methodically, the left-most letter is the slowest-changing one. It is chosen first, and held constant until all possible ways of filling in the remainder of the answer are found. Then we go back to the start, try a different choice for the first position, and hold this constant while the different ways of completing the remainder of the answer are found. This continues until the list is exhausted.

This process is not unlike the way Prolog tries to find all possible answers to a compound query. If a query has two subgoals, the first one is attempted first. Once a solution to the first part is found (perhaps setting variables in the process), these variables are held constant until all possible solutions to the second part are found. Then the system retraces its steps, goes back to the first subgoal again, and tries for a different solution to this first part. This second attempt at the first part could result in new values being given to the variables. Then, with these new variable values held constant, all possible solutions to the second part are found. This process continues until no new solutions to the first part can be found, at which point the system answers no. The process by which the system retraces its steps and goes back to a previous subgoal looking for a possible new solution to it, is called *backtracking*.

To illustrate this process, consider a query which asks for all possible pairs of employers and candidates for any vacancy as a secretary:

```
?-has_vacancy (Employer, secretary),
     trained_as (Candidate, secretary).
```

The answer to this query will be all combinations of the variables Employer and Candidate (and note that the query introduces them in that order), such that the given condition holds. The system finds these combinations by taking each solution to the first subgoal in turn; then, for each of these, it finds all solutions to the second subgoal. Since there are just two solutions to the first part (Employer = harvard, and Employer = prentice_hall), the combinations will be found in two groups: first, all those with Employer = harvard; then those with Employer = prentice_hall:

```
{ First, with Employer = harvard, find all solutions to
  trained_as (Candidate, secretary)                    }

  Employer = harvard
  Candidate = elizabeth;
  Employer = harvard
  Candidate = mary;

{ Now with Employer = prentice_hall, find all solutions to
  trained_as (Candidate, secretary)                    }

  Employer = prentice_hall
  Candidate = elizabeth;
  Employer = prentice_hall
  Candidate = mary
```

2.4   A geography database

Figure 2.1 shows a map of part of Europe, though it is considerably simplified, and even inaccurate. It contains some details of regions, seas and mountains. The information on the map is to be stored as a Prolog program, so that anyone can ask questions of the system about what is on the map. The sorts of simple question to be asked might be:

- What regions are there?
- What mountains are there, and which regions are they in?
- Which regions border another given region?
- Which seas border a given region?

The information given by the map can be stated by simple Prolog relationships. It is good practice to do this in two stages:

(i) Define the basic components on the map.
(ii) Define the relationships between all these basic components.

Firstly, the basic components. There are three different types of component — regions, seas and mountains. The fact that France, say, is a region (rather than a sea or a mountain) could be written as:

```
region (france).
```

This needs to be done for all the regions on the map, giving the following facts:

```
region (france).
region (germany).
region (switzerland).
region (austria).
```

```
region (italy).
region (sicily).
```

The seas can similarly be defined, using a predicate *sea*:

```
sea (english_channel).
sea (mediterranean).
sea (adriatic).
```

Figure 2.1 *Map of Europe*

Lastly, the mountains need to be defined:

```
mountains (alps).
mountains (pyrenees).
mountains (apennines).
```

So far, only the basic components have been defined; there is nothing to say which region borders which, or which region contains which mountains. This information is added to the program by defining the various relationships which exist between the basic components. The relationships which the map shows are:

- The fact that one region borders another.
- The fact that a sea touches the coast of a particular region.
- In which region each mountain range is contained.

The fact that, say, France borders Germany can be stated in Prolog as:

```
borders (france, germany).
```

But since Prolog does not realise that this naturally means that Germany borders France, a second fact must be added to this effect:

```
borders (germany, france).
```

This needs to be done for all eight borders, giving sixteen facts in total:

```
borders (france, germany).
borders (france, switzerland).
borders (france, italy).
borders (germany, france).
borders (germany, switzerland).
borders (germany, austria).
borders (switzerland, france).
borders (switzerland, germany).
borders (switzerland, austria).
borders (switzerland, italy).
borders (austria, germany).
borders (austria, switzerland).
borders (austria, italy).
borders (italy, france).
borders (italy, switzerland).
borders (italy, austria).
```

We also need to define which seas touch the coast of which region:

```
touches_coast_of (english_channel, france).
touches_coast_of (mediterranean, france).
touches_coast_of (mediterranean, italy).
touches_coast_of (mediterranean, sicily).
touches_coast_of (adriatic, italy).
```

Finally, we define which regions contain which mountains:

```
contains (france, pyrenees).
contains (switzerland, alps).
contains (italy, apennines).
```

This has defined all the basic information which the map gives. So it should now be possible to extract this information by asking queries. Here are some examples:

(i) *What seas are there?* In Prolog, this would be formulated as:

```
?-sea (Sea).
```

and would produce the following answers (if all answers were requested):

```
Sea = english_channel;
Sea = mediterranean;
Sea = adriatic;
no
```

(ii) *What mountains are there, and which region is each range in?* In Prolog, this is:

```
?-mountains (Mountains),
   contains (Region, Mountains).
```

Actually, the first of these subgoals might be regarded as being redundant, since mountains can only be contained in a country anyway. As it stands, the query would produce the following response (if all solutions were asked for):

```
Mountains = alps
Region = switzerland;
Mountains = pyrenees
Region = france;
Mountains = apennines
Region = italy;
no
```

Other information which is not stated explicitly can be worked out from the database of facts, by asking compound queries:

(iii) *Which regions are islands?* The program does not state this explicitly, but it can be worked out logically, if we assume that an island is a region which has no border with another region. If a region has no land borders, then:

```
?-borders (Region, _).
```

should fail. However, to get something which *succeeds* if there are no
borders rather than fails, we have to make use of the built-in Prolog
not predicate, where:

```
not (fact)
```

succeeds if *fact* fails, and vice versa. Therefore, to find all islands, we
would present the query:

```
?-region (Island),
  not (borders (Region, _)).
```

This would produce the answer:

```
Island = sicily;
no
```

A final note on Prolog's matching of queries

The Prolog system answers queries by matching patterns between the
query and the stored database (the program). This matching process is
methodical and mechanical, and does not require the system to *understand*
what either the program or the query means. For instance, given the fact:

```
likes (fred, elizabeth).
```

the system has no idea who or what fred and elizabeth are, and does
not have the faintest notion what likes means. It merely notes that a
relationship called likes exists between two objects called fred and
elizabeth, in that order. Answering queries can be done without
understanding, though. For instance, someone in Iceland might write
some facts from a saga as the following Prolog clauses:

```
elska (helgi, unn).
elska (hrafnkel, bergthora).
elska (helgi, bergthora).
```

If the following query was presented:

```
?-elska (X, bergthora).
```

then, irrespective of what this all means, and without appreciating the
blood that may have been spilt because of the situation described by these
facts, it should be fairly obvious that the answer will come back:

```
X = hrafnkel;
X = helgi;
no
```

Because no attempt is made to understand what is input, Prolog is quite prepared to accept what we would regard as either a mistake, or as utter nonsense. For instance, if by mistake we entered the fact:

```
fred (likes, elizabeth).
```

then Prolog would interpret this blindly as stating in English that:

likes fred elizabeth

(whatever it means *to fred* something). Or, it would happily accept the following facts:

```
nosh (gurble, nurdle).
jikker (snuffit, yaxxen).
```

Prolog's simple built-in pattern matching reasoning process can carry on regardless in the face of information which to us would be totally confusing.

EXERCISES

1 A database of hobbies

The fact that a person has a certain hobby, or enjoys a particular activity, can be expressed in Prolog by defining a relation such as:

```
enjoys ( person, activity )
```

For instance, the fact that Fred enjoys playing baseball would be stated as:

```
enjoys (fred, baseball).
```

Take an imaginary group consisting of the following people:

Margaret, Nancy, Jane, Denis, Ronald and Robert

These individuals enjoy various activities selected from the following list:

music, soccer, baseball, reading, travel and painting

For each of these hypothetical people, draw up a list of activities which you imagine them to enjoy. Write each of these as a Prolog fact, stating that the person enjoys that particular activity or hobby. Naturally, a person can have more than one hobby. Define up to three or four activities for each person.

How would you then ask questions such as the following in Prolog:

(i) *What hobbies does Robert have?* Ask if there is an activity such that Robert enjoys it, and if so, what is it. You can get all his activities by repeatedly asking for more solutions.

(ii) *Do Ronald and Margaret have any common interests?* Ask if there is an activity which they both enjoy.

(iii) *Is there anyone who enjoys soccer and baseball, but does not enjoy music?*

2 A family tree

Relationships within a family can be defined in terms of the following simple predicates:

```
married_to ( person1, person2 )
child_of ( person1, person2 )
male ( person )
female ( person )
```

which, respectively, state that:

person1 is married to *person2*
person1 is a child of *person2*
person is male
person is female

For instance, a database of a family with parents Denis and Margaret, and son Mark, would be defined by the facts:

```
male (denis).
male (mark).
female (margaret).

married_to (denis, margaret).
married_to (margaret, denis).

child_of (mark, denis).
child_of (mark, margaret).
```

Now consider the following well-known family tree shown in Figure 2.2. Using only the above predicates, write the information in this tree as a Prolog program.

How would you then ask the following questions:

(i) *Who are the children of Anne?*

(ii) *Who are the parents of William?*
(iii) *What brothers does Edward have?* A brother of Edward is someone who has the same parents as Edward does, and who is also male.
(iv) *Who are the grandparents of Peter?* A grandparent is a parent of a parent.

This exercise will be taken up in more detail in Chapter 3.

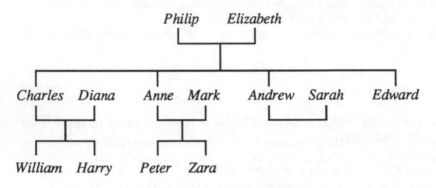

Figure 2.2 *Family tree*

3 Another geography database

We want a program which does the same job for a map of the British Isles as was done for the earlier European geography database.

The information included on the physical map of the British Isles is as follows:

- For the sake of argument, call the regions England, Scotland, Wales, Ulster, Eire, and Isle of Man.
- The seas which touch the coasts of the British Isles are the English Channel, the North Sea, the Irish Sea and the Atlantic.
- The mountains to be included are: the Pennines (in England), the Mournes (in Ulster), and the Grampians (in Scotland).

Define the basic components on the map, and then the relationships between all these basic components. Once the program is complete, ask the following queries:

(i) *What regions are there?*
(ii) *Which regions are land-locked?* A land-locked region has no coastline.
(iii) *Which regions have a coastline and mountains?*

3

General rules in Prolog

So far, all our Prolog statements have been blunt statements of fact, which state that something is true, all the time, and under all circumstances. Unfortunately, life is not quite as simple as this. Often in real life, a statement is true only under certain circumstances. To make such a statement in Prolog, we have to be able to qualify the statement by giving the conditions under which it holds. This chapter is about how to do this by writing general rules in Prolog.

3.1 Writing Prolog rules

In English, something which is conditional (as opposed to an unconditional fact) is often stated in the terms:

> *such-and-such is true* **if** *some condition holds*

Let us say, for instance, that an employer is looking for a person with certain *qualities*, rather than with a specific training. For example, if NASA happens to be looking for someone who is clear-thinking and accurate, then this information might be written as the rule:

> *NASA might employ someone* **if**
> *that person is clear-thinking and accurate*

In Prolog, a statement can be made to be conditional by qualifying it using *if*, written as ':-' in Prolog, followed by the conditions. For instance, our general rule about who NASA might employ would be written as:

```
might_employ (nasa, X) :-
      clear_thinking (X),
      accurate (X).
```

A rule of this form states that provided the condition(s) on the right-hand side hold, then the conclusion on the left is valid. A fact as described in Chapter 2 is just a special case of a Prolog rule, being one with no conditions. In general, the right-hand side can contain several conditions, all of which must be true for the conclusion to be valid:

conclusion : – *condition₁* , *condition₂* , ...

Whenever a query is asked, the system makes use of the rules, and follows them logically to work out the answer. Thus, if the question is asked:

```
?-might_employ (Employer, joe).
```

then the system selects the first rule for `might_employ`. If this happens to be the above rule about NASA, then the system interprets this rule as saying: to check if NASA might employ Joe, check first if Joe is clear-thinking; if so, check if he is accurate. Only if both conditions (or subgoals) are satisfied does the query succeed. Note that the reasoning process is just the same as when answering a compound query.

Likewise, a candidate might also wish to place certain conditions on a prospective employer. For instance, to state that Michael is prepared to work for an employer only if the employer is hi-tech and small, we could define the Prolog rule:

```
prepared_to_work_for (michael, Employer) :-
    hi_tech (Employer),
    small (Employer).
```

Rules can themselves be used to define other rules, such as in:

```
match_possible (Employer, Candidate) :-
    might_employ (Employer, Candidate),
    prepared_to_work_for (Candidate,
                            Employer).
```

Checking a goal of this kind can lead to a chain of reasoning which gets deeper each time another rule is referenced. For instance, for the goal:

```
?-match_possible (nasa, michael).
```

the first subgoal will be tackled first:

```
might_employ (nasa, michael)
```

This subgoal is checked by selecting the rule which defines the conditions under which NASA might employ someone. Thus, this subgoal will in turn be broken down into two further subgoals:

```
     clear_thinking (michael)
```
and
```
     accurate (michael)
```

Provided each of these succeeds, the system will then proceed to the second of the two original subgoals:

```
     prepared_to_work_for (michael, nasa)
```

This is likewise broken down into its two constituent subgoals, by applying the rule which defines who Michael is prepared to work for. This chain of reasoning can become quite involved, and difficult to follow. So it will help to trace the checking of a goal by drawing it out systematically. The following is one way of doing this:

```
match_possible (nasa, michael)  ?

     might_employ (nasa, michael)  ?

          clear_thinking (michael)  ?
          -  succeeds
          accurate (michael) ?
          -  succeeds

     prepared_to_work_for (michael, nasa)  ?

          hi-tech (nasa) ?
          -  succeeds
          small (nasa) ?
          -  fails
     -  fails
-  fails
```

3.2   Alternative clause definitions

We have already noted that Prolog allows us to build a compound query or goal using 'and' (written using a comma). Often, though, we wish to write clauses using 'or', such as:

Joe likes Mary or Elizabeth

More generally, let us say we want to make statements of the form:

a likes b or c

One way of achieving this is to make two separate statements:

```
a_likes_b_or_c (A, B, C) :- likes (A, B).
a_likes_b_or_c (A, B, C) :- likes (A, C).
```

It should be clear that each of these statements on its own is true, although not necessarily the *whole* truth. If A likes B, then the conclusion that A likes either B or C is certainly valid, as the first clause states. If A likes C, then it likewise follows that A likes B or C (which is what the second clause says). There is no need to think that we have to state everything about a relationship in a single clause.

From the system's point of view, if it is asked:

```
?-a_likes_b_or_c (joe, mary, elizabeth).
```

then it will try to apply the first definition of the relation a_likes_b_or_c, and check that:

```
likes (joe, mary)
```

If Joe does not like Mary, then this will fail. But all is not lost, because the system will now look for alternative definitions of the predicate a_likes_b_or_c, and only admit failure when all definitions have been exhausted. Thus, the next attempt will be to try the second definition of a_likes_b_or_c, which will be broken down into a check that:

```
likes (joe, elizabeth)
```

If this succeeds, then the initial query will succeed.

In summary, then, the effect of an 'or' is achieved by writing separate clauses for each different case, where a clause can be either a fact or a conditional rule. During query answering, the different clauses will be tried in the order in which they were defined, until one succeeds or until all have been tried.

The fact that different definitions of the same predicate are tried in a fixed order means that the earlier definitions have some sort of priority. This usually shows up only when the clause is used to find a solution rather than to check one. For instance, if we want to find someone who likes either Mary or Elizabeth, we would ask:

```
?-a_likes_b_or_c (Person, mary, elizabeth).
```

and wait for the first answer. Since the first definition to be tried will always be:

```
likes (Person, mary)
```

we are more likely to be given someone who likes Mary, rather than Elizabeth, even though the question probably intended no bias. When generating all solutions by repeatedly typing semicolon, the order of the definitions is shown up in the order of the different answers. This feature is not usually a problem, and indeed can be used to advantage, as the next example shows.

3.3   Example: employment agency revisited

Let us change the ground rules a little for our simple employment agency program. Instead of looking only for someone who has already been trained in a particular skill, employers may also be prepared to do the training themselves. They are therefore also on the look-out for candidates who have the potential to become the sort of person the employer needs.

An employer's position might be stated by saying that, if the employer has a vacancy, then the first preference is for someone who *has* been trained in the required skill; but if no trained person is available, then someone who has the necessary personal qualities would be acceptable. This means that there are really two alternative conditions under which a person is acceptable to an employer to do a given job. One condition is that the candidate has already been trained; the other is that the candidate has not been trained, but could be. In Prolog, we will have a separate clause to cover each of these alternative cases. And since the first case is preferred, then the clause for the first case is defined first. We want to define a predicate:

```
acceptable (Candidate, Employer, Skill)
```

which states the conditions under which Candidate is acceptable to Employer to do a job requiring the given skill. The two alternative definitions of this predicate are therefore as follows:

```
acceptable (Candidate, Employer, Skill) :-
    has_vacancy (Employer, Skill),
    trained_as (Candidate, Skill).

acceptable (Candidate, Employer, Skill) :-
    has_vacancy (Employer, Skill),
    not (trained_as (Candidate, Skill)),
    could_be_trained_as (Candidate, Skill).
```

The predicates has_vacancy and trained_as would be defined by simple statements of fact, and not as conditional rules. The remaining predicate:

```
could_be_trained_as (Candidate, Skill)
```

is however conditional: it depends on whether or not Candidate has the necessary personal qualities to learn Skill. To define the predicate could_be_trained_as fully, it is necessary to define the required qualities for each skill separately. This might give us the following set of clauses:

```
could_be_trained_as (X, secretary) :-
      accurate (X),
      literate (X),
      out_going (X).

could_be_trained_as (X, programmer) :-
      clear_thinking (X),
      accurate (X),
      intelligent (X).

could_be_trained_as (X, driver) :-
      co_ordinated (X),
      hard_working (X).

could_be_trained_as (X, salesman) :-
      out_going (X),
      hard_working (X).

could_be_trained_as (X, author) :-
      imaginative (X),
      literate (X).
```

Selecting a clause

Note that when a program contains multiple clauses defining a predicate like this, and the system is given the goal:

```
could_be_trained_as (X, Y)
```

then it will automatically begin by trying to apply the first definition (thus looking to see if X could be trained as a secretary). If this does not succeed, it will try subsequent definitions in order, until one succeeds or until all the definitions have been tried.

Note that applying a rule (as distinct from just matching a fact) takes place in two stages, both of which must succeed:

(i) The goal is matched with the left-hand side of the rule. The objects in the goal must all match the templates in the rule. This is the same unification process as used in matching the goal with unconditional facts. Thus, an attempt to match:

```
could_be_trained_as (X, driver)
```

with the first definition of `could_be_trained_as` will fail, because `driver` does not match `secretary`.

(ii) If the left-hand side matches, then the conditions are checked, in order.

Let us now complete our employment agency program. To obtain a complete program for our revised employment agency, we now only have to add factual information about what vacancies there are, who has been trained as what, and the personal qualities of each of the candidates. The following set of facts might describe a typical situation:

```
has_vacancy (harvard, secretary).
has_vacancy (prentice_hall, author).
has_vacancy (ibm, salesman).
has_vacancy (hertz, driver).
has_vacancy (nasa, programmer).
has_vacancy (prentice_hall, secretary).

trained_as (michael, programmer).
trained_as (fred, taxidermist).
trained_as (mary, secretary).

accurate (elizabeth).
accurate (mary).
accurate (michael).
accurate (fred).

out_going (michael).
out_going (mary).
out_going (elizabeth).

co_ordinated (joe).

hard_working (mary).
hard_working (joe).
hard_working (michael).

clear_thinking (elizabeth).

intelligent (mary).

imaginative (michael).
```

The following are some example queries which could be presented to this program, and the answers which would be produced assuming all solutions are requested:

(i) *Who is acceptable to Hertz?* In Prolog:

```
?-acceptable (Candidate, hertz, _).

Candidate = joe;
no
```

(ii) *To which employers is Michael acceptable, and for which jobs?* In Prolog:

```
?-acceptable (michael, Employer, Job).

Employer = nasa
Job = programmer;
Employer = ibm
Job = salesman;
no
```

(iii) *Are any employers competing for the same candidate?*

```
?-acceptable (Candidate, E1, _),
  acceptable (Candidate, E2, _),
  not (E1 = E2).
```

If we know from the outset that this is likely to be a reasonably common query, then it would be better to define who an employer's competitors are *within the program*. The following is a predicate which states the conditions under which an employer E1 has a competing employer E2 over a given candidate:

```
competitor (E1, E2, Candidate) :-
    acceptable (Candidate, E1, _),
    acceptable (Candidate, E2, _),
    not (E1 = E2).
```

The query which a user has to enter is now much simpler. For instance, to discover which employers might be fighting over Elizabeth, the query would be asked:

```
?-competitor (E1, E2, elizabeth).

E1 = harvard
E2 = prentice_hall;
E1 = prentice_hall
E2 = harvard;
no
```

Note here the effect of the Prolog system being unable to recognise that different orderings of the same employers are not really new solutions. Prolog cannot recognise that the relation `competitor` is symmetric.

This approach of defining extra predicates to facilitate common queries is not only more convenient for the user: it is also safer. Where possible, any relations which are likely to be required by a user should be identified beforehand, and defined within the program like this.

3.4 Example: family relationships

Being a member of a family automatically involves a person in all kinds of different relationships: child, parent, grandchild, brother, sister, cousin, mother-in-law, great-great-grandchild, and so on. We will show how these relationships can be defined in Prolog. As an example, consider the family tree for the well-known family mentioned in Exercise 2 at the end of the previous chapter:

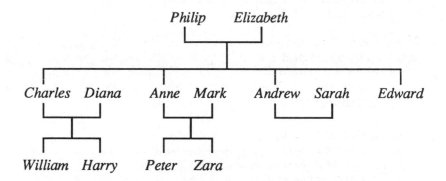

The relationship between, say, Charles and Philip can be defined by the Prolog fact:

```
child_of (charles, philip).
```

which states that Charles is a child of Philip. But the relationship between Charles and Philip is also one of father-to-son; so perhaps we should define this further relationship by another, separate fact:

```
parent_of (philip, charles).
```

Logically, there should be no need to state explicitly who is a parent of who if we have already defined the `child_of` relationship, since one can always be inferred from the other. The general rule for working out the `parent_of` relationship given the `child_of` relationship can be written as the following Prolog rule:

```
parent_of (X, Y) :- child_of (Y, X).
```

This states that if Y is a child of X, then X is a parent of Y. Note that we could equally well have chosen to define `parent_of` as a set of facts, and then defined `child_of` in terms of `parent_of`. There is no real difference. In general, some relationships will be 'fundamental', being specified explicitly by facts; the rest can be deduced from other relationships, and are written as general rules. The fundamental relationships necessary to define a family tree are:

```
child_of (X, Y)      { defines 'vertical' relationships }
married_to (X, Y)    { defines 'horizontal' relationships }
```

Since these are genderless relations, we will also need to know whether a person is male or female. This will enable us to distinguish a father from a mother, for instance. This requires two further predicates:

```
male (X)
female (X)
```

All these predicates must be defined as specific facts for each person in the family:

```
male (philip).
male (charles).
female (elizabeth).
married_to (philip, elizabeth).
married_to (elizabeth, philip).
child_of (charles, philip).
child_of (charles, elizabeth).
...
```

All other relationships can be defined in terms of these basic predicates. We now consider some further relationships.

(i) *Fathers and mothers*. The predicate `parent_of` makes no distinction between father or mother; it really means `father_or_mother_of`. We can define a father to be a male parent, and a mother to be a female parent:

```
father_of (X, Y) :- parent_of (X,Y),
                    male (X).

mother_of (X, Y) :- parent_of (X,Y),
                    female (X).
```

(ii) *Brothers and sisters.* A *sibling* is the term used for a brother or sister. We might define siblings as people who have a common parent:

```
sibling_of (X, Y) :- parent_of (P, X),
                     parent_of (P, Y),
                     not (X = Y).
```

Note the need for the last condition (not (X = Y)). This prevents someone being defined as a sibling of themselves. This definition actually has a drawback: if a query asks for *all* siblings of X and Y, then each pair will be duplicated, since each is related by two different parents. So if in our example family we asked for the siblings of Edward:

```
?-sibling_of (edward, X).
```

the answer would be:

```
X = charles;
X = anne;
X = andrew;
X = charles;
X = anne;
X = andrew;
no
```

The definition as it stands really defines all combinations of X, Y *and* P such that the right-hand side is satisfied, and there are two values of P for each X and Y. An improvement would be to define a sibling as someone who shares the same father and mother:

```
sibling_of (X, Y) :- father_of (F, X),
                     mother_of (M, X),
                     father_of (F, Y),
                     mother_of (M, Y),
                     not (X = Y).
```

Now, a brother is a male sibling, and a sister is a female one:

```
brother_of (X, Y) :- sibling_of (X, Y),
                     male (X).
sister_of (X, Y)  :- sibling_of (X, Y),
                     female (X).
```

(iii) *Aunts, uncles and cousins.* An aunt is the sister of a parent; an uncle is the brother of a parent:

```
aunt_of (X, Y)  :- parent_of (P, Y),
                   sister_of (X, P).
```

```
uncle_of (X, Y) :- parent_of (P, Y),
                   brother_of (X, P).
```

A cousin is the child of an aunt or an uncle. To handle the 'or', we have the option either of writing two clauses for a cousin, or of defining an intermediate relation:

```
aunt_or_uncle_of (X, Y) :- aunt_of (X, Y).
aunt_or_uncle_of (X, Y) :- uncle_of (X, Y).
```

with a cousin then defined as:

```
cousin_of (X, Y) :- child_of (X, P),
                    aunt_or_uncle_of (P, Y).
```

The latter solution is probably better, since it may prove useful to have the relation aunt_or_uncle_of in defining other relationships.

We could now check, for instance, that Andrew is the uncle of Harry by asking:

```
?-uncle_of (andrew, harry).
```

or ask for all cousins of William, by:

```
?-cousin_of (william, Cousin).
```

This latter query would produce the response:

```
Cousin = peter;
Cousin = zara;
no
```

(iv) *Grandchildren and grandparents.* Since a grandchild is the child of a child, its Prolog definition is quite straightforward:

```
grandchild_of (X, Y) :- child_of (X, P),
                        child_of (P, Y).
```

This in turn can be used to define the grandparent relationship:

```
grandparent_of (X, Y) :- grandchild_of (Y,X).
```

Having these various relationships defined as part of the program greatly simplifies the user's task of formulating queries. Things should always be made as simple and convenient as possible for the user!

3.5   Recursive rules

We already have Prolog rules for `child_of` and `grandchild_of`. But what about subsequent generations? Suppose we want to define the conditions under which someone is a *descendant* of someone else. How do we define a descendant? We might be tempted to say that a descendant is a child, or a grandchild, or a great-grandchild, and so on:

```
descendant_of (X, Y) :- child_of (X, Y).
descendant_of (X, Y) :- grandchild_of (X, Y).
descendant_of (X, Y) :- great_grandchild_of
                                       (X, Y).
...
```

where each generation would need to be defined separately:

```
grandchild_of (X, Y) :-
               child_of (X, Z),
               child_of (Z, Y).
great_grandchild_of (X, Y) :-
               child_of (X, Z),
               grandchild_of (Z, Y).
great_great_grandchild_of (X, Y) :-
               child_of (X, Z),
               great_grandchild_of (Z,Y).
...
```

Not only is this approach very tedious, but we must also stop sooner or later. This means that we will have defined descendants only up to a fixed number of generations, and so will not really have solved the problem completely. A clue to a better solution is to notice a pattern in the definition of each generation above: note that each new generation is defined in terms of the previous one. So consider a new definition of what is meant by a descendant:

> *The descendants of Y are Y's children, along with their descendants*

Note that we have defined *descendant* in terms of itself. A rule which is defined in terms of itself is called *recursive*. To turn this into a Prolog rule, it needs to be rephrased to state when X is a descendant of Y:

> *X is a descendant of Y either if X is a child of Y,*
> *or if X is a descendant of a child of Y*

This can now be formulated as a Prolog predicate:

```
descendant_of (X, Y) :- child_of (X, Y).
descendant_of (X, Y) :- child_of (C, Y),
                        descendant_of (X, C).
```

If the following query was asked, to find descendants of Elizabeth as defined by the previous example of a family tree:

```
?-descendant_of (X, elizabeth).
```

then the answer would be:

```
X = charles;
X = anne;
X = andrew;
X = edward;
X = william;
X = harry;
X = peter;
X = zara;
no
```

When a recursive use of a rule is encountered by the system, it is treated just like a reference to any other rule. This is illustrated by tracing the behaviour of the system when given the query:

```
?-descendant_of (harry, elizabeth).
```

Using our earlier notation for tracing, this would give the following:

```
descendant_of (harry, elizabeth) ?
```

{ Try first clause: }
```
        child_of (harry, elizabeth) ?
        - fails
```

{ Try again with second clause for descendant_of: }

```
        child_of (C, elizabeth) ?
        - succeeds, setting C to charles

        descendant_of (harry, charles) ?

                child_of (harry, charles) ?
                - succeeds
        - succeeds
- succeeds
```

Terminating recursion

Somehow when one sees a recursive definition such as descendant_of, there is a nagging doubt in the back of the mind: might the system not go on for ever, trying to answer a recursive query? There certainly are times when this can happen. Suppose, for instance, that a person called Dave likes anyone who likes him. We could write this in Prolog as:

```
likes (dave, X) :- likes (X, dave).
```

But suppose there are *two* indecisive people like this: Dorothy also likes anyone who likes her:

```
likes (dorothy, X) :- likes (X, dorothy).
```

If two indecisive people like this come into contact, problems can arise. So suppose the query is now asked: *does Dave like Dorothy?*

```
?-likes (dave, dorothy).
```

So Dave says he will like Dorothy if she likes him; and Dorothy says she will like Dave if he likes her. If we are not careful, we could end up oscillating between one and the other, waiting for one of them to make up their mind one way or the other. As humans, we are intelligent enough to recognise when we are in an infinite cycle like this, and can stop the process. But the Prolog system is not, and it will blindly alternate between asking if Dave likes Dorothy and asking if Dorothy likes Dave. So no answer would come back to this query: the computer would just sit there. In practice, it will eventually come back with a message to the effect that it has run out of memory.

There is no danger of this situation arising when working out descendants, however. To find the descendants of a person, we work down through that part of the family tree headed by the person in question. Since a person cannot be the parent of one of their ancestors, we are always going down the tree, and there can be no connections back to people higher up the tree. We must therefore eventually reach the bottom of the family tree, and stop that line of search. This can be seen from the definition of `descendant_of`: note that both clauses in its definition start with `child_of`. Eventually the system reaches the bottom of the tree, where a person has no children. At this point, `child_of` will fail. So because there are no 'loops' or cycles in a family tree, the process will eventually stop.

3.6   Example: a power distribution network

Electricity consumers in a district are supplied with electricity from an electricity generating station. This power is distributed from the station to the various consumers through a system of transformers, as shown in the diagram:

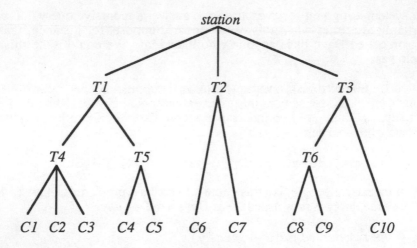

C1 to C10 are consumers; T1 to T6 are transformers. From time to time, one of the transformers may malfunction, or may need to be taken out of service temporarily. If this should happen, the management would naturally wish to know which consumers will be affected. We will therefore write a simple Prolog program to help the management in their task.

The fact that one point in the distribution network directly feeds another point is shown on the diagram by a line connecting the two points. In Prolog, this same information could be defined by the fact:

```
feeds (X, Y).
```

Thus, the fact that the station feeds transformer T1 is defined by:

```
feeds (station, t1).
```

Doing this for every connection gives a representation of the entire network:

```
feeds (station, t1).
feeds (station, t2).
feeds (station, t3).
feeds (t1, t4).
feeds (t1, t5).
feeds (t3, t6).
feeds (t4, c1).
feeds (t4, c2).
feeds (t4, c3).
feeds (t5, c4).
feeds (t5, c5).
feeds (t2, c6).
```

```
feeds (t2, c7).
feeds (t6, c8).
feeds (t6, c9).
feeds (t3, c10).
```

Since we intend to ask questions which distinguish between consumers, transformers and the station, this information should also be defined:

```
generator (station).
transformer (t1).
transformer (t2).
transformer (t3).
transformer (t4).
transformer (t5).
transformer (t6).
consumer (c1).
consumer (c2).
consumer (c3).
consumer (c4).
consumer (c5).
consumer (c6).
consumer (c7).
consumer (c8).
consumer (c9).
consumer (c10).
```

The predicate feeds refers only to *direct* connections. But one point can feed or supply another *indirectly*. Note, for instance, that T1 supplies T4 and T5 and consumers C1 to C5. We therefore wish to define a predicate:

```
supplies (X, Y)
```

which states when point X supplies point Y either directly or indirectly. The conditions under which X supplies Y can be expressed as follows:

> *X supplies Y <u>either</u> if X feeds Y directly,*
> <u>*or*</u> *if X feeds directly a point which supplies Y*

Note that this is a recursive definition. It is a relatively simple matter to express this in Prolog:

```
supplies (X, Y) :- feeds (X, Y).
supplies (X, Y) :- feeds (X, Point),
                   supplies (Point, Y).
```

If we now want to know which consumers will be affected by a fault at one point in the network, we can use supplies to find out. For instance, if transformer T1 goes down, the query would be:

```
?-supplies (t1, C), consumer (C).
```

which would yield the answer:

```
C = c1;
C = c2;
C = c3;
C = c4;
C = c5;
no
```

The second condition in the query avoids the appearance of intermediate transformers in the list of points supplied by T1.

Alternatively, a consumer (C8, say) may ring up to report a power loss. To find out which of the transformers could be responsible for the power cut, the query could be asked:

```
?-supplies (T, c8), transformer (T).
```

which asks for which transformer supplies C8. This would produce the answer:

```
T = t6;
T = t3;
no
```

Again, we can be sure that this recursive definition of `supplies` will not cause the system to get into an infinite cycle, provided the network has no *feedback*. Feedback would be indicated by having a line going back up the diagram; this would form a closed path, which could be followed *ad infinitum*. Whenever the system reaches a consumer, `supplies` will fail, thus ending that line of recursive checking. A consumer does not feed any other point.

3.7   Review of Prolog's matching strategy

When the user presents the Prolog system with a query, the system takes the query as a 'theory' and tries to prove it logically, rather like a detective would. It either *fails* to find any possible solution, or *succeeds*. We call something which Prolog sets out to prove a *goal*. The process of trying to prove a goal is called *evaluating* the goal.

A goal may contain variables which are initially free, such as in:

```
?-acceptable (Employer, Candidate).
```

In evaluating a goal, the system tries to find a replacement of the free variables which would make the goal succeed. This happens when the variable is matched with a specific object.

Evaluating goals

Given a goal involving a predicate, such as:

```
could_be_trained_as (elizabeth, Skill)
```

the system will evaluate the goal by trying each of the definitions in the program of that predicate, in the order in which they appear in the program. Each definition is applied in turn, until one succeeds or until all definitions have been tried. An attempt to apply a program rule to solve a goal takes place in two stages:

(i) The arguments in the goal are matched, or unified, with the arguments in the definition. For instance, matching the above goal with the rule:

```
could_be_trained_as (X, secretary) :- ...
```

will set the variable X in the goal to elizabeth, and Skill in the definition to secretary. If the definition is just a fact, with no further conditions, then the goal succeeds only if this matching is successful. If the definition is a conditional rule, then the system proceeds to phase (ii).

(ii) The right-hand side of the rule is used to break the goal down into a number of subgoals. These subgoals are evaluated in turn, from left to right, either until all have succeeded, or until one fails. If all have succeeded, the goal succeeds. If one subgoal should fail, however, causing the application of this rule to fail, the system will not give up entirely. Instead, it will search for the next definition of the same subgoal, and apply this. Only if no definition succeeds does the goal fail. Thus when a subgoal fails, the system's strategy is to go back to the nearest point at which there was an alternative, and try this alternative path. In this way, the system *searches* for solutions until it finds one or until it fails altogether. For instance, consider the following definition which defines the sort of person Elizabeth likes:

```
likes (elizabeth, X) :- tall (X), rich (X).
```

together with the following clauses which state that someone is rich either if they are a programmer or a teacher:

```
rich (X) :- programmer (X).
rich (X) :- teacher (X).
```

Given the goal:

```
likes (elizabeth, michael)
```

(where Michael is a tall teacher who cannot program), then a trace of the system's behaviour in evaluating this goal would be:

```
likes (elizabeth, michael) ?
```

> ```
> tall (michael) ?
> ```
> *- succeeds*
>
> ```
> rich (michael) ?
> ```
>
> > ```
> > programmer (michael) ?
> > ```
> > *- fails*

{ At this point, go back to the nearest point where there was an alternative which has not yet been considered; so try the next definition of *rich* }

> > ```
> > teacher (michael) ?
> > ```
> > *- succeeds*
>
> *- succeeds*

- succeeds

Prolog therefore performs a systematic search for solutions. The direction of this search depends on the structure of the rules which are applied. Think of the structure of rules which are defined in terms of subgoals as having a structure like the 'tree' shown below:

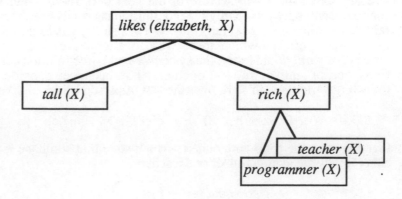

For a goal to succeed, all branches (representing conditions) must succeed. A branch with several different definitions appears in the diagram as:

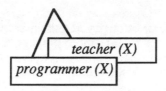

When a branch has alternatives, only one has to succeed for that branch to succeed. In this notation, when one alternative branch does fail, Prolog merely goes back up the tree one level, and sees if there are any more alternative paths it could have followed down the tree. If this attempt should fail, then the system will step back up yet another level, and so on, until either a successful path is found, or until all paths have been tried and failed. The process of stepping back up the tree structure in an attempt to find a successful path is called *backtracking*.

It is this systematic and relentless search for a solution which gives the Prolog system its logical reasoning ability. Its search strategy is certainly logical enough, but it is not particularly intelligent.

EXERCISES

1 Compatible interests

Using a predicate:

    enjoys (*person, activity*)

make up and define a database of facts for an imaginary group which states who enjoys doing what. As in Exercise 1 in Chapter 2, the people in this group are:

Margaret, Nancy, Jane, Denis, Ronald and Robert

and the activities which they enjoy are selected from:

music, soccer, baseball, reading, travel and painting

If you did Exercise 1 in Chapter 2, your answer will do nicely for this.
    Now, define a Prolog predicate:

    compatible1 (X, Y)

which succeeds if the two people X and Y have at least one common activity which they enjoy. Then define:

```
compatible2 (X, Y)
```

which succeeds only if X and Y enjoy at least *two* common activities.

Suppose some activities require three players, and you wish to know if there are three members of the group who enjoy one of these activities, so that they can do it together. Write a rule:

```
three_for (Activity) :- ...
```

which succeeds only if at least three people in the group enjoy the given activity.

2   More family relationships

Using the predicates defined earlier in the chapter, write Prolog rules to define the following relationships:

```
nephew_of (X, Y) :- ...
neice_of (X, Y) :- ...
mother_in_law_of (X, Y) :- ...
brother_in_law_of (X, Y) :- ...
```

3   Management structures

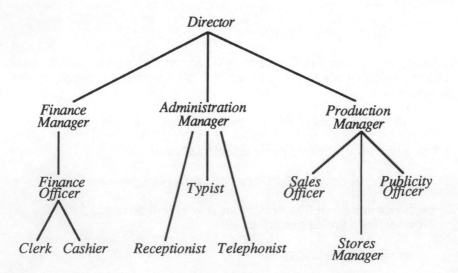

The diagram shows the management structure for a firm. The fact that one person works for another is indicated in the diagram by one person being directly below the other. This fact will be stated in Prolog using the predicate:

```
works_for (X, Y)
```

Using this predicate, write a set of Prolog facts which defines the above management structure.

Now write Prolog rules for the following:

(i) *X is the (immediate) boss of Y.*
(ii) *X is under Y in the firm* (either directly or indirectly).
(iii) *X is over Y in the firm* (either directly or indirectly).

4

Structured objects

So far, all the objects which we have been using have been indivisible, with no internal structure (like `fred`, or `station`, or `jaguar`). But some of the more interesting and useful objects in life actually consist of several simple objects or pieces of information, grouped together into a single unit. Consider the following three examples.

(i) *Dates*

A date, such as 20th January 1988, has three parts:

- the day   (a number between 1 and 31)
- the month (one of January, ... , December)
- the year   (a positive — or perhaps negative — number)

A date is therefore a divisible object with three components.

(ii) *Meals*

A full meal usually has at least three courses:

- starter
- main course
- dessert

Thus a meal is an object with several components. A meal is particularly interesting, not least because each of its components can itself have structure. A main course, for example, typically has meat, vegetables and potatoes.

(iii) *Library catalogue entry*

An entry in a library catalogue is a description of a book. This description may perhaps be held on a card in a card index. It contains selected information about the book. A simple entry might contain the following for each book:

- author
- title
- classification (indicating where to find it on the shelves)

Together, these pieces of information describe a book. Thus, as far as this catalogue is concerned, a book is merely a structured object with three components.

If we want our Prolog programs to be able to use objects such as these, we must have a way of representing and processing structured objects in Prolog. This chapter describes how this is done.

4.1 Describing structured objects in Prolog

When faced with real-life objects which have to be represented and processed in Prolog, there are two fundamental steps to be taken:

(i) Identify the *kind* of object it is: what general group or category of object does it belong to ? (Is it a book? or a date? or what?)
(ii) Identify the *components* which objects of this kind have. What pieces of information have to be held to tell us all we need to know about this kind of object?

Given this information, a structured object is then described in Prolog as:

object-kind(component₁ , component₂ , ...)

Let us take each of the three example objects mentioned above: dates, meals and library index entries. We will see how each could be represented in Prolog, given this general pattern.

(i) A date will have the general structure in Prolog:

date *(day, month, year)*

Some examples are:

```
date(31, january, 1988)
date(25, december, 1990)
```

Sometimes it is convenient to think of a structured object diagrammatically. A date object could be drawn in the format:

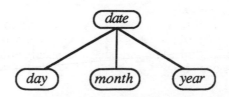

Thus, the first actual date above would be represented as:

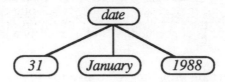

(ii) A meal will have the general form:

    meal(*starter, main-course, dessert*)

The problem arises now about how each of these three sub-
components is to be represented, since each can have structure of its
own. As a general rule, if we have a number of simple objects (such
as steak, peas and chips) which we want to group together to
form a more complex object (a main course), then these are
represented in the same structured way — the components are grouped
in brackets, and given the name of the general category of such
objects:

    main_course(steak, peas, chips)

Any structured object like this can be included as a component of another
object, and there is no limit on the depth or complexity of structure:

    meal(starter(melon, ginger),
         main_course(steak, peas, chips),
         dessert(peaches, cream))

A diagram can be particularly useful for thinking about objects with this
type of more complex hierarchical structure. The above meal, for instance,
would be drawn as follows:

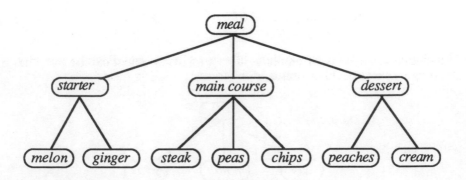

Strictly speaking, structured objects of a particular kind do not necessarily always have to have exactly the same number of components. In practice, though, they usually do; indeed, some versions of Prolog make this a requirement. Also, if necessary, a structured object can have just one component. Thus, the following are equally valid objects, from a Prolog point of view at least:

```
starter(prawn_cocktail)
main_course(chicken, sausage, bacon, tomato,
                     corn, chips, pineapple)
meal(starter(soup),
     salad,
     main_course(hamburger),
     dessert(apple_pie, cream),
     dessert(ice_cream),
     drink(coffee))
```

An unstructured object such as fred is really a special case of a structured object with no components: the name of the object corresponds to the object kind. Note too that there is a difference between a structured object with just one component, and the single component on its own; for example, the two objects:

```
starter(soup)
soup
```

are regarded in Prolog as two totally different objects: one is of kind starter, the other of kind soup.

(iii) An entry in our simple library catalogue has three components, and describes an object of kind book:

book (*author*, *title*, *classification*)

Some typical entries in a catalogue could be represented in Prolog as follows:

```
book(shakespeare, macbeth, qt_13_s35)
book(dickens, oliver_twist, qt_49_d23)
```

The diagrammatic way of representing a structured object can be a useful stepping stone between a real-life object and a Prolog description of that same object. In general, the object which ends up in Prolog as:

object-kind(component$_1$, component$_2$, ...)

will be drawn as:

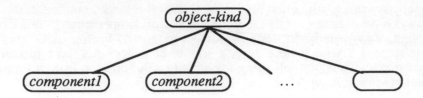

Using objects in clauses

A structured object can be used in the same way, and in the same places, as any other object. For instance, if we need to define when people were born, we could write a Prolog predicate:

```
date_of_birth (person, date)
```

where *date* will be a structured object as described above:

```
date_of_birth (fred,
               date(1, february, 1957)).
date_of_birth (shakespeare,
               date(26, april, 1564)).
```

The fact that, say, Gary eats a particular meal could be defined by the predicate:

```
eats (gary, meal(starter(cereal),
            main_course(bacon, eggs))).
```

Or, to state that a particular book is in the library catalogue, we need a predicate:

```
in_library (book)
```

where *book* is a structured object in the above format:

```
in_library (book(stowe,
            uncle_toms_cabin,
            qv_14_s8)).
in_library (book(shakespeare,
            romeo_and_juliet,
            qr_49_s35)).
```

Simple queries have the same structure as before. To ask when Shakespeare was born, the query would be:

```
?-date_of_birth (shakespeare, D).
```

which would produce the answer:

```
D = date(26, april, 1564)
```

Or, to see if anyone has been recorded as having been born on Christmas day 1987, we would ask:

```
?-date_of_birth (P, date(25, december, 1987)).
```

Or, the entire library catalogue could be listed by asking for all solutions to the query:

```
?-in_library (B).
```

4.2 Accessing components of a structured object

Our use of structured objects in clauses and queries to date has required us to use only complete objects, such as entire dates or meals. Obviously, there will be a need to pick out individual components of a structured object; we will want, for example, to pick out just the author of a book, or the month of a date. Likewise, we will want to build up a structured object, given its components.

The way to pick out a component of a structured object is to match the actual object with a template — a dummy structured object of the same kind whose components can be variables. For instance, matching the two objects:

```
date(23, may, 1953)
date(D, M, Y)
```

will set the day D to 23, the month M to may, and the year Y to 1953. This pattern matching takes place when Prolog applies a clause to solve a goal. Two structured objects match, or unify, only if they are of the same kind, and if each of their corresponding components match.

Suppose we want a predicate which selects the month from a given date:

```
month (date, month)
```

This is written as:

```
month (date(_, M, _), M).
```

which will succeed if each of the following holds:

(i) The date supplied in the first position is a date with three components.

(ii) The second component of the supplied date is called M. It does not matter what the first and third components are.

(iii) The second argument of this predicate is either the same object as M, or can be made to be the same.

Note: The use of the same variable in two different positions in a clause or in a structured object means that the objects which occupy those positions must be identical.

Now, if the system is given the goal:

```
?-date_of_birth (shakespeare, D),
   month (D, Mon).
```

it will first set D to:

```
date(26, april, 1564)
```

and then proceed to the second subgoal, substituting the value of D:

```
month (date(26, april, 1564), Mon)
```

Applying the definition of month given above, this specific date is matched with the template in the clause:

```
month (date( _, M, _), M).
```

This could be made to succeed if the variable Mon is set to april. Since pattern-matching effectively *tries* to make things match, this is what will happen. The answer to the above query will therefore be:

```
D = date(26, april, 1564)
Mon = april
```

This predicate can be used either to select the month component, or to check it. For instance, given the query:

```
?-date_of_birth (fred, D),
   month (D, november).
```

this will fail, given that Fred's date of birth was stated previously to be 1st February 1957. This is because the second component of the date D (February) and the supplied month M do not match. This tells us that Fred was not born in November.

A similar approach enables us to define predicates which select the day or the year of a given date:

```
day (date(D, _, _), D).
year (date(_, _, Y), Y).
```

A few more example queries illustrate the use of component selection:

(i) *Who was born in January?*

```
?-date_of_birth (P, D), month (D, january).
```

(ii) *Was anyone born in the same year as Shakespeare?*

```
?-date_of_birth (shakespeare, date(_, _, Y)),
   date_of_birth (P, date(_, _, Y)),
   not (P = shakespeare).
```

(iii) *Does a particular date fall on Christmas day?* We can define a predicate which succeeds if a given date is Christmas day (in any year), and fails otherwise:

```
christmas (date(25, december, _)).
```

Example: a library catalogue

We have seen that a library catalogue can be defined in Prolog by a list of facts:

```
in_library (book(stowe,
                 uncle_toms_cabin,
                 qv_14_s8)).
in_library (book(shakespeare,
                 romeo_and_juliet,
                 qr_49_s35)).
. . .
```

A user can look up this catalogue by asking simple Prolog queries:

(i) *Do you have* Macbeth *by Shakespeare, and if so, what is its classification?*

```
?-in_library (book(shakespeare,
                   macbeth, Class)).
```

(ii) *Do you have* Uncle Tom's Cabin *(I do not know who wrote it)?*

```
?-in_library (book(Author,
                   uncle_toms_cabin, Class)).
```

This will return the author and the classification.

(iii) *What books do you have by Dickens?*

```
?-in_library (book(dickens, Title, _)).
```

This will return only titles, and not their classification.

(iv) *Are there any books with the same title, but different authors?*

```
?-in_library (book(A1, T, _)),
   in_library (book(A2, T, _)),
   not (A1 = A2).
```

A major advantage of this solution is that there is no need to maintain separate Author and Title catalogues. Also, by including another component which gives information on the *subject* of a book, a user could search for books by subject, thus giving a Subject catalogue. The drawback with this solution is that the search which is initiated by a query could be very lengthy, since each entry in the catalogue has effectively to be scanned individually.

We could also attempt to computerise the lending records maintained by the library, by defining a set of clauses which state which books are out on loan:

```
on_loan (book, borrower, date-due)
```

At any instant, the program would contain a set of definitions of on_loan, such as:

```
on_loan (book(stowe,
               uncle_toms_cabin, qv_14_s8),
         robinson,
         date(21, november, 1988)).
on_loan (book(shakespeare,
               romeo_and_juliet, qr_49_s35),
         wilson,
         date(7, september, 1988)).
   ...
```

Given a complete set of definitions like this, queries such as the following could be asked:

(i) *What books has Jones borrowed?*

```
?-on_loan (Book, jones, _).
```

(ii) *Who has at least two books out?*

```
?-on_loan (Book1, Borrower, _),
   on_loan (Book2, Borrower, _),
   not (Book1 = Book2).
```

(iii) *Is* Romeo and Juliet *out on loan?*

```
?-on_loan (book(_, romeo_and_juliet, _),
           _, _).
```

This will return just a yes/no answer, and ignore all the associated
details of the book and the borrower.

To keep this program up to date, the program would have to be modified
every time a book was either borrowed or returned. When a book is taken
out, a new clause must be added to the program, by defining another clause
for on_loan. This should give details of the book, the borrower, and the
return date. When a book is returned, the clause which had earlier been
defined must be deleted from the program. These changes at present have
to be performed using the program editing facilities provided by your
Prolog system, which is rather unsatisfactory. In the next chapter, we will
see how this can be done more conveniently.

4.3   Lists in Prolog

Most of the structured objects encountered so far have two properties:

 (i) Their components can be of different types. For example, a date has
     numbers and a *month* as its components.
(ii) For a given kind of object, the number of components is usually fixed.
     For instance, there are three for a date, or for a book.

There are often times, however, when the objects we are working with do
not have these properties. It is common to have a *list* of components, and it
is often the case that these components are of the same kind (though this
need not necessarily be the case). In such a list, there is no predefined limit
on the number of components. For example, the interests of a person
might be written as:

> *tennis, baseball, sailing, reading, ludo*

Or, a book could be classified by subject by giving a list of keywords
(rather than a single keyword, which would be rather inadequate). This
book which you are now reading might have the list of subjects:

> *computing, programming, Prolog*

In neither of these examples is there any predefined number of elements which we would expect to find in the list; there might be many, or there might even be none.

In Prolog, because lists are a very common form of structured object, there is a special notation to represent them. A list in Prolog is a grouping of any number of objects. For greater flexibility, the objects do not necessarily all have to be of the same kind. A list of objects in Prolog is written as:

> [*element₁, element₂, element₃, ...*]

A list with no elements in it (the *empty* list) is written as:

> [ ]

Note the two main differences between this notation and the usual notation for structured objects: square brackets are used instead of round brackets, and there is no need to specify the initial kind of object — Prolog can see that it is a list, by the square brackets. Thus, the two example lists above would be represented in Prolog as follows:

```
[tennis, baseball, sailing, reading, ludo]
[computing, programming, prolog]
```

When working with lists whose length is not known beforehand, in English we would usually write such a list as, say:

> *tennis, ...*

where '...' represents the remaining elements in the list. In Prolog, instead of writing '...', a different notation is used to represent the rest of the list:

```
[tennis| X]
```

The object `tennis` at the front of this list is called the *head* of the list. The variable X is the list of remaining elements in the list (called the *tail*). It is a Prolog list in its own right, and may have any number of elements, including zero. In a list written using the dividing token '|', everything up to the divider is an element; after the divider must come a list (perhaps a variable). If this is representing the above list of interests, then the variable X is a list which has the value:

```
[baseball, sailing, reading, ludo]
```

A Prolog list can be matched in several different ways, depending on how far along the list we put the '|' divider. Thus the list:

```
[tennis, baseball, sailing, reading, ludo]
```

can be matched in many different ways:

        [tennis| X]
where X = [baseball, sailing, reading, ludo]

or   [tennis, baseball| X]
where X = [sailing, reading, ludo]

or   [tennis, baseball, sailing| X]
where X = [reading, ludo]

or   [tennis, baseball, sailing, reading| X]
where X = [ludo]

or   [tennis, baseball, sailing, reading, ludo| X]
where X = []

or   [tennis| [baseball, sailing, reading, ludo]]

or   [tennis| [baseball| [sailing| [reading|
                              [ludo| []]]]]]

Note that there is a difference between:

        [tennis]

and

        tennis

The first object is a list, consisting of one element followed by a tail which is the empty list; the second is not a list at all.

We are now in a position to define some simple predicates on lists:

(i)   A predicate which will succeed only if the given list is *empty* (or can be made to be the empty list, if it is a free variable):

        emptylist ([]).

(ii) A predicate which will succeed only if the given list has *exactly one element*:

        one_element ([_]).

(iii) A predicate for testing if a list has *at least three elements*:

        at_least_three_elements ([_, _, _| _]).

This will attempt to match the supplied list with a list which has three elements at the start followed by a 'tail' list. This tail list will just be the empty list if the supplied list has exactly three elements. A list with fewer than three elements will fail to match.

4.4   Processing lists

With lists, there is now a problem which we did not really have before: how to process an object with an unknown number of components. Suppose we require a predicate which tests if all the people in a list are rich:

```
all_rich (List)
```

If we try to decompose the list completely and name each component separately, this would require a clause for each size of list: no elements, one element, two elements, and so on:

```
all_rich ([]).
all_rich ([P1]) :- rich (P1).

all_rich ([P1, P2]) :- rich (P1),
                       rich (P2).

all_rich ([P1, P2, P3]) :- rich (P1),
                           rich (P2),
                           rich (P3).
    ...
```

But there is the obvious problem that 'and so on' is not good enough. The key to programming the 'and so on' part is to use *recursion*, because we discovered earlier that recursive rules do not put a predefined limit on the processing.

If we think of a list more generally as:

person1, ...

and now ask if each person in the list is rich, an obvious strategy is first to check *person1*, and if this succeeds, then proceed to check the rest of the list. In the above example, the rest of the list is represented by '...'. In Prolog, a non-empty list can be decomposed in exactly this way by writing it as:

```
[Person1| Tail]
```

The only list which cannot be written like this is the empty list. When decomposed, `Person1` is the first element on the list (the *head* of the list);

`Tail` is the list of all remaining people. The conditions under which a list can be said to be all rich could be rephrased as follows. Remember that the list might be either empty or non-empty:

> *A list is all rich if*
> > <u>*either*</u>   *the list is empty*
> > <u>*or*</u>   *the list has the structure [Person1 | Tail]*
> >   *and Person1 is rich*
> >   *and the list Tail is all rich.*

In Prolog, it is now straightforward to define this as two separate clauses, using recursion:

```
all_rich ([]).
all_rich ([Person1| Tail]) :- rich (Person1),
                              all_rich (Tail).
```

For instance, consider a trace of the query:

```
?-all_rich ([elizabeth, joe]).
```

If both Elizabeth and Joe are stated individually to be rich, then a trace of the evaluation of this query would be as follows:

```
all_rich ([elizabeth, joe])   ?
```

  { first clause fails; try the second clause for `all_rich`: }
  { second clause initially sets }
  { Person1 = elizabeth, Tail = [joe] }

```
        rich (elizabeth)   ?
```
        - succeeds

```
        all_rich ([joe])   ?
```

    { first clause fails; try second clause: }
    { second clause initially sets }
    { Person1 = joe,   Tail = [] }

```
            rich (joe)   ?
```
         - succeeds

```
            all_rich ([])   ?
```
         - succeeds   { by first clause }

    - succeeds

   - succeeds

On a more general note, if a list is to be tested for having all elements with a particular property, a suitable predicate would have the form:

```
all_have_property ([]).
all_have_property ([Head| Tail]) :-
                    has_property (Head),
                    all_have_property (Tail).
```

4.5   List processing examples

There are some fairly standard ways in which lists are used. In this section, we develop Prolog rules for a few problems which occur frequently in different contexts.

Membership testing

Suppose we want to know if the list of a person's interests contains one particular interest. A predicate:

```
contains (List, Interest)
```

is required, which will succeed only if Interest is one of the elements in List. Thus the two goals:

```
contains ([tennis, art, judo], judo)
contains ([tennis, art, judo], music)
```

should succeed and fail respectively.

Whenever a problem involves processing a list, it should always be broken down into two simpler cases: when the list is empty, and when it is not. Now consider our problem for each of these two cases:

(i) Can an empty list contain a given interest? Obviously not, so contains must fail for any empty list. We do not need to write a special clause which states this: if none of the clauses eventually written can apply to the empty list, then failure is automatic.

(ii) Under what conditions can a non-empty list contain the given interest? There are two possibilities: either the list starts with Interest, or the rest of the list contains Interest. Note that this latter case involves a recursive use of contains. These two cases can be written as separate clauses in Prolog:

```
contains ([Interest| _], Interest).
contains ([_| Tail], Interest) :-
            contains (Tail, Interest).
```

This is the complete definition of `contains`. Note that neither clause allows for the possibility of the list being empty. Now follow a typical use of `contains`, in answering the query:

```
?-contains ([tennis, reading], reading).
```

The system will initially try to apply the first definition of `contains`; but this will fail, since `tennis` and `reading` are not the same object. So the system tries again, with the second definition. Doing the initial pattern matching, the goal becomes:

```
contains ([tennis| [reading]], reading)
```

which is reduced by the right-hand side of the rule to the subgoal:

```
contains ([reading], reading)
```

For this new goal, the system temporarily suspends consideration of the first goal, and starts afresh on this subgoal, beginning as usual with the first definition. This time, the pattern-matching succeeds, since the list `[reading]` starts with `reading`. The subgoal succeeds immediately, resulting in the overall goal being successful. If the list had not in fact contained the given interest, the second clause would have reduced the list of interests to the point where `Tail` was the empty list. This would result in failure. This trace of the behaviour is summed up more concisely as follows:

```
contains ([tennis, reading], reading)   ?
```
{   first clause fails; try second clause: }
{   second clause initially sets `Tail` = `[reading]` }

```
        contains ([reading], reading)   ?
        - succeeds      { by first clause }
```

- *succeeds*

This predicate `contains` is very useful, and can be used for searching lists of any sort in many different applications. It is worth remembering.

Finding a route

Consider again the simple geography database developed in Chapter 2, in which borders between regions were defined:

```
borders (france, germany).
borders (germany, france).
```

```
borders (france, switzerland).
...
```

The problem we now consider is that of either finding or checking a route between two regions. A route will just be a list of regions. We therefore require a predicate:

```
route (C1, C2, Route)
```

which will succeed if it is possible to travel by land from C1 to C2 by visiting the regions in the list Route in order. Thus:

```
?-route (france, austria, R).
```

should succeed, returning the answer:

```
R = [france, germany, switzerland, italy,
      austria]
```

However, the following should fail:

```
?-route (france, sicily, R).
```

In general, the strategy in going from C1 to C2 will be to take just a single step at a time. In other words, the route from C1 to C2 consists of a single step to an intermediate bordering region C3, followed by a route from C3 to C2. Unfortunately, this presents a problem (which has been carefully avoided up to now). If we set out from C1 trying different paths until we arrive at C2, it would be possible to get into a situation where we go round in circles: say, France to Germany, Germany to France, France back to Germany, and so on. The Prolog system on its own will not recognise that it has been to France before. To get a safe solution, we will therefore have to check ourselves that the intermediate region C3 has not already been visited. The easiest way to check this is to carry around the list of regions visited so far, and check that C3 is not a member of this list. This requires a new predicate which has got four arguments instead of three:

```
safe_route (C1, C2, Route, So_far)
```

This states that Route will be a path between C1 and C2 such that it does not contain any elements of the list So_far. So_far is the list of regions visited so far prior to C1 (but not including C1). This predicate is defined for two cases: when we have already arrived, and when we have not.

```
safe_route (C1, C1, [C1], _).
safe_route (C1, C2, [C3| R], So_far) :-
        borders (C1, C3),
        not (contains (So_far, C3)),
```

```
                     safe_route (C3, C2, R,
                                  [C3| So_far]).
```

The initial predicate `route` can now be defined in terms of `safe_route`, noting that at the start no regions have been visited:

```
          route (C1, C2, Route) :-
                  safe_route (C1, C2, Route, []).
```

Common elements

It is sometimes necessary to take two lists, and work out the list of common elements. The common elements are those which are on both lists. For instance, in checking if two people are compatible, it would be useful to find the list of their common interests. This operation is sometimes called finding the *intersection* of the two lists. For the two lists:

```
          [tennis, baseball, reading, ludo]
          [ludo, music, baseball, judo, art]
```

the list of common interests is:

```
          [baseball, judo]
```

The relationship between these three lists will be defined by a predicate:

```
          intersection (List1, List2, Intersection)
```

Building the list `Intersection` can be done by working through `List1` element by element. For each element, if it is a member of `List2`, then it is also a member of `Intersection`. Again, to define this sort of list processing in Prolog, it is always best to separate the two cases of when the list is empty and when it is non-empty.

(i) If `List1` is empty, there are no common elements:

```
          intersection ([], _, []).
```

(ii) Write the non-empty `List1` as `[Head|Tail]`. Either `Head` is on `List2` or it is not. If it is, `Head` should be added to the list of common elements. The remaining common elements (called `T`, say) are those which are common to both `Tail` and `List2`. These can be found using `intersection` recursively:

```
          intersection ([Head|Tail], List2, [Head|T]):-
                  contains (List2, Head),
                  intersection (Tail, List2, T).
```

If Head is not a common element, then all the common elements must just be common to Tail and List2:

```
intersection ([Head| Tail], List2, T) :-
            not (contains (List2, Head)),
            intersection (Tail, List2, T).
```

The three clauses for intersection define the predicate completely. Again, it is a useful predicate to be familiar with.

EXERCISES

1 American football teams

At the start of a game of American football, when commentators read out the names of the 11 players on a team, they usually structure the starting defensive team description as follows:

- *name of the team*
- *linemen*   (3 players)
- *linebackers*   (4 players)
- *defensive backs*   (4 players)

For instance, the following might be the starting defensive formation of one possible team:

<u>*Seattle Seahawks*</u>

Green   Nash   Bryant

Gaines   Young   Bosworth   Jackson

Brown   Easley   Moyer   Hunter

Thus, a complete team description is a structured object with four components, some of which are themselves structured objects.

Draw the structure of the Seattle Seahawks team in the diagrammatic form used earlier in the chapter:

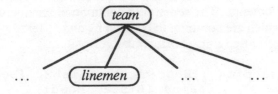

Then define the format of a Prolog structured object which represents an American football team structured in this way. Define Prolog object descriptions of the Seattle Seahawks, and of one other team of your choice (real or imaginary).

Now let us say that the fact that a particular team is in a final is defined by the predicate:

> in_final (*team-description*)

There should obviously be two clauses for this predicate, since exactly two teams will be in a normal final. Assuming that these clauses have been defined, we could for instance ask for both team descriptions to be displayed by asking for all solutions to the query:

> ?-in_final (Team).

How would you now ask the following queries in Prolog:

(i) *What are the names of the teams playing in the final?*
(ii) *Who are the eight defensive backs in this final?*
(iii) *Is Nash the central lineman on either of the teams in the final?*

2 Subject catalogue

To give some indication of what a book is about, a list of keywords could be included in the description of a book developed earlier in the chapter. For instance, the subject of this book might be described by the Prolog list:

> [computing, programming, prolog]

First, extend the earlier description of a book to include a slot for this information:

> book (*author, title, classification, subject*)

Choose a few books from your bookshelf, and define a small library catalogue. This should now contain subject information, and invented classifications. Do this using the predicate:

> in_library (*book*)

Given a database of this form, how would you ask the following queries in Prolog:

(i) *What books are there in the library on the subject of sport?*
(ii) *What is the classification of books on history?*
(iii) *What books in the library are on the subjects computing, programming or computers?*

In formulating your queries, feel free to make use of the predicates `contains`, `intersection`, etc., developed earlier in the chapter.

3 More list operations

Here are two further general list processing predicates to add to `contains` and `intersection`. Both the predicates below will require recursion.

Deleting from a list. Write a predicate:

```
delete (List_in, Element, List_out).
```

which states that `List_out` is `List_in` with any occurrences of `Element` removed. If there are none to start with, `List_out` and `List_in` will be the same; if there are several occurrences of `Element` in `List_in`, all should be deleted.

In defining this predicate, break the problem down into the by-now-familiar set of more specific cases:

* `List_in` is empty, *or*
* `List_in` is non-empty, *and*
  * Head of `List_in` is `Element`, *or*
  * Head of `List_in` is *not* `Element`.

Appending two lists. Write a predicate:

```
append (List1, List2, List3).
```

which states that appending `List2` to the end of `List1` gives `List3`. This is commonly used to join one list on to the end of another. You will find it useful to approach the problem by working through `List1` element by element, until it is empty.

4 Simple sentences

The words in an English sentence can be held as a Prolog list, such as:

```
[the, black, cat, sat, on, the, mat]
[fred, is, a, wally]
```

Let us restrict ourselves to those English sentences which have a very specific and simple pattern, such as:

the dog bit the man
the boy ate a banana

The general structure of these sentences is as follows:

> *article noun verb article noun*

An article is a word such as 'the', or 'a'. The first two words always give the subject of the sentence; the third word is always the verb; and the fourth and fifth words are the object. Assume we are always dealing with sentences which have this simple structure. Thus, sentences can be represented in Prolog by lists which always have five elements.

Write a simple Prolog program which defines a number of sentences, using the predicate:

> sentence *(list-of-words)*

For instance:

```
sentence ([a, man, kicked, a, dog]).
sentence ([the, dog, chased, the, man]).
sentence ([the, man, climbed, a, tree]).
. . .
```

How would you now formulate queries in Prolog to ask the following questions:

(i) *Which sentence has 'chased' as the verb?*
(ii) *Which sentence has 'the man' as the subject?*
(iii) *Are there two sentences such that the subject of one is exactly the same as the object of the other?* An example of this is:

```
[the, man, climbed, a, tree]
[the, dog, chased, the, man]
```

Here, the two-word phrase 'the man' constitutes the subject and object respectively.

5

Other Prolog facilities

In this chapter, we conclude our introduction to the language Prolog by considering some additional facilities which Prolog provides: arithmetic, input and output, and program updating. The precise details of how these facilities are provided tend to vary a little from one version of Prolog to another, so it is best to check out the details before trying to use these features on your own system.

5.1   Arithmetic

Most of our examples so far have not even used numbers, let alone arithmetic. This is not because Prolog is unable to do arithmetic; it is more to show that you do not have to be a mathematician to write Prolog programs. Nevertheless, most useful Prolog programs will usually involve *some* arithmetic.

Basic operations

Calculations can be performed on numbers in Prolog using a set of simple operations, such as addition and subtraction. An *arithmetic expression* is a more general term for a calculation which could involve several operations. The following are the basic arithmetic operations available in Prolog. In the description, X and Y could be either numbers or expressions, but must not be free variables:

(i) *Addition:*   X + Y

(ii) *Subtraction:*   X − Y

(iii) *Multiplication:*   X * Y

(iv) *Division:*   X / Y
The result is the whole number part of a division; thus 5/2 gives the answer 2.

(v) *Remainder:*   X mod Y
The result is the remainder after dividing X by Y; thus 13 mod 5 would give the answer 3.

Evaluating an expression

Prolog has a built-in predicate which causes an expression to be evaluated:

> *variable* is *expression*

If *variable* is a free variable, then its value is set to the value of the expression; otherwise the predicate will succeed only if the existing value of the variable is the same as the value of the expression. The following queries illustrate the operation of *is*:

```
?-X is 2 * 8 + 5.
X = 21

?-X is 12, X is 10.
no

?-X is 12, Y is 3 * X - 1.
X = 12
Y = 35

?-X is 12, Y is 2 * X, X is Y - X.
X = 12
Y = 24
```

When evaluating an expression which contains several operations, such as:

```
X - Y + Z
```

someone might interpret this as saying:

> *take X, and subtract from it the sum of Y and Z*

rather than the more usual interpretation:

> *subtract Y from X, and add Z to the result*

Prolog will evaluate an expression from left to right; but to avoid possible confusion, it is best to use brackets to indicate the order in which calculations are to be carried out:

```
(X - Y) + Z
```

We have already seen that an expression should not contain free variables. For instance, suppose X is a free variable in the statement:

```
42 is 6 * X
```

It would of course be possible to make this statement true, simply by giving X the value 7. So the statement is certainly not wrong. However, most Prolog systems will not allow a statement of this kind for the purposes of finding X.

Comparisons

It is often necessary to compare two numbers, perhaps to see if one is less than another. Prolog provides six ways of comparing numbers. In all six operations, the values being compared must be expressions, or variables which already have a value — but *not* free variables:

X < Y   succeeds if the value of X is *less than* the value of Y
X > Y   succeeds if the value of X is *greater than* the value of Y
X =< Y   succeeds if the value of X is *less than or equal to*
                     the value of Y
X >= Y   succeeds if the value of X is *greater than or equal to*
                     the value of Y
X =\= Y   succeeds if the value of X is *not equal to* the value of Y
X =:= Y   succeeds if the value of X is *equal to* the value of Y

Note that there now seem to be two different ways of testing if two objects are equal, since we could write conditions such as:

```
X = Y
X =:= Y
```

The difference is that the first equality 'tries' to make the two sides equal, perhaps by giving values to variables in the process. In the second case, both variables *must* already have values.

An example which uses comparisons is a simple predicate which succeeds if a given value N is within certain specified bounds. These bounds will be called Lower and Upper. For instance, the goals:

```
in_range (10, 1, 100)
in_range (5, 5, 8)
```

should succeed, but both the following goals should fail:

```
in_range (0, 1, 10)
in_range (20, 1, 10)
```

For in_range to succeed, two conditions must be satisfied: N must be greater than or equal to Lower, and N must also be less than or equal to Upper:

```
in_range (N, Lower, Upper)  :- N >= Lower,
                               N =< Upper.
```

Example: days in a month

Let's say we want a predicate which defines the number of days in a particular month. Based on the old rhyme *'Thirty days hath September, April, June and November ...* ', we might begin by defining a single clause for each month:

```
days_in_month (31, january).
...
days_in_month (30, november).
days_in_month (31, december).
```

This would be fine if it were not for February, because the number of days in February depends on the *year*. If the year is a leap year, then February has twenty-nine days; otherwise it has twenty-eight. This means that the predicate days_in_month must also take the year into account:

```
days_in_month (number-of-days, month, year)
```

This states that there are *number-of-days* days in the given *month*, in the given *year*. For all months, except February, the number of days is independent of the year, in which case the year can actually be ignored. For February, the number of days is twenty-nine if we are in a leap year, or twenty-eight otherwise:

```
days_in_month (31, january,  _).
days_in_month (29, february, Y) :-
                          leap_year(Y).
days_in_month (28, february, Y) :-
                          not (leap_year(Y)).
days_in_month (31, march,    _).
days_in_month (30, april,    _).
days_in_month (31, may,      _).
days_in_month (30, june,     _).
days_in_month (31, july,     _).
```

```
days_in_month (31, august,     _).
days_in_month (30, september, _).
days_in_month (31, october,    _).
days_in_month (30, november,   _).
days_in_month (31, december,   _).
```

This leaves us with the task of defining the predicate:

```
leap_year (Y)
```

which should succeed only if Y is a leap year. Even this is not as simple as seeing if Y is divisible by 4, though, since if Y is a century (e.g. 1900 or 2000), it is a leap year only if divisible by 400. When we come to express these rules in Prolog, it will be convenient to have a predicate which succeeds if one number X is exactly divisible by another number Y. This will be the case when the remainder after dividing X by Y is zero:

```
divisible_by (X, Y) :- 0 is X mod Y.
```

Now we can define a leap year:

```
leap_year (Y) :- divisible_by (Y, 400).
leap_year (Y) :- not (divisible_by (Y, 100)),
                 divisible_by (Y, 4).
```

Example: arithmetic with lists

It is common to have lists of numbers which require arithmetic. For instance, we might want to add up a list of numbers, or find their average, or sort them. Here are a few examples.

(i) *Length of a list.* A predicate is required:

```
length (List, L)
```

which specifies the conditions under which L is the length of the list List. The length of a list is the number of elements in it. As with list processing predicates, two cases should be treated separately: when the list is empty, and when it is not. Firstly, how do we define the length of an empty list? An empty list has no elements, so a single statement does the job:

```
length ([], 0).
```

For a non-empty list, we can say that the length of the list:

```
[_| Tail]
```

is certainly one more than the length of the list `Tail`. This will in fact define the length of the complete list, since the length of `Tail` can be found by applying exactly the same rule (recursively). This gives the following complete definition of `length`:

```
length ([], 0).
length ([_| Tail], L)  :- length (Tail, T),
                          L is T + 1.
```

To illustrate the operation of this predicate, consider the query:

```
?-length ([tennis, ludo], L).
```

The following trace of the evaluation of this goal shows how it returns the value 2:

```
length ([tennis, ludo], L)   ?
```

{ first clause fails; try the second clause of `length`:   }
{ second clause initially sets `Tail` = `[ludo]`   }

```
    length ([ludo], L)   ?
```

   { first clause fails; try second clause: }
   { second clause initially sets `Tail` = `[]`   }

```
        length ([], L)   ?
        - succeeds { by first clause },  returning value 0

        L is 0 + 1 = 1
```

   - *succeeds*, returning value 1

```
    L is 1 + 1 = 2
```

- *succeeds*, returning value 2

(ii) *Sum of a list*. To add up all the numbers in a list, a predicate can be written following the pattern of `length`. We first note that the sum of a list with no elements is just zero. Otherwise, the sum of a list is found by adding the head to the sum of the tail list. This gives a very similar form:

```
sum ([], 0).
sum ([Head| Tail], S)  :- sum (Tail, T),
                          S is Head + T.
```

As an example of the operation of this predicate, the query:

```
?-sum ([12, 14, 5, 1, 10], Total).
```

would succeed, returning the answer:

```
Total = 42
```

(iii) *Minimum of a list.* This case differs from length and sum in that the minimum of an empty list is undefined. The simplest case is when the list has just one element, in which case the minimum is just that element:

```
minimum ([Min], Min).
```

For any other list:

```
[Head| Tail]
```

we have first to find the minimum of the list Tail, and compare this with Head. This final comparison will have to choose the minimum from just two numbers, for which a separate predicate can be written:

```
min_of2 (Number1, Number2, Minimum).
```

This states that Minimum is the smaller of Number1 and Number2. It can be defined by:

```
min_of2 (N1, N2, N1) :- N1 < N2.
min_of2 (N1, N2, N2) :- N1 >= N2.
```

This now enables us to define the predicate minimum completely:

```
minimum ([Min], Min).
minimum ([Head| Tail], Min) :-
        minimum (Tail, T),
        min_of2 (Head, T, Min).
```

For instance:

```
?-minimum ([21, 34, 19, 44, 19, 18, 50], Min).
```

would produce the answer:

```
Min = 18
```

5.2   Output in Prolog

Interacting with a Prolog program was intended primarily to be by question and answer. This is the main form of input and output in Prolog. But this is not really sufficient to write general-purpose programs which are easy to use. The technical phrase for being easy to use is *user-friendly*. For this purpose, more sophisticated input and output are obviously required. Prolog provides some simple built-in predicates for this, but these extensions do not fit completely naturally into a reasoning-based language like Prolog. In this section, we first consider output.

Prolog provides one main predicate for displaying an object on the screen, and one to help tidy up the display.

(i) *Writing an object*

```
write (object)
```

This predicate always succeeds, and in the process displays the object on the screen. Thus, output is something of a side-effect. Writing a variable which has been bound to an object will display that object. You should avoid attempting to write a free variable! For instance:

```
?-X is 5 * 9, write (X).
```

would display the answer 45. But because the system will itself respond with the answer to this query in the usual way, what actually appears on the screen is:

```
45X = 45
```

The first 45 is displayed as a result of evaluating `write(X)`. Note that the system will not automatically take a new line, so the answer to the query is displayed immediately after this. This is where the X = 45 comes from in the above response. To overcome this problem, another built-in predicate is provided for output.

(ii) *Taking a new line*

```
nl
```

The predicate *nl* stands for *new line*. This predicate always succeeds, and takes a new line in the process. To tidy up the output from our query above, we could rephrase the query as:

```
?-X is 5 * 9, write (X), nl.
```

This would now produce the answer:

```
45
X = 45
```

Note, in passing, one problem with output in Prolog: an output cannot be *undone*. Once something has been displayed in the process of evaluating a query, then it remains there whether or not the query ultimately succeeds. Consider, for instance:

```
?-X is 5*9, write (X), nl, X = 90.

45
no
```

String objects

So far, the only kind of unstructured objects we have met are either named objects (such as january or tennis) or number objects (such as 1 or 1988). For output purposes, to add text which helps the appearance of what is displayed, it is useful to be able to write any sort of text. For this purpose Prolog provides an additional type of unstructured object — so-called *string* objects. A string is just a list of characters enclosed in quotes. The following are examples of strings:

```
'a typical string'
'UPPER_CASE_STRING'
'  '
'... the previous one was just a space'
'1988'
```

The system effectively ignores what is inside the quotes, except to store it; it makes no attempt to analyse the string. Thus, for instance, the last example is not confused with a number object, and the second example is not interpreted as a variable. String objects are treated by the system just like any other kind of object. A string can appear anywhere a named object or a number object or a variable could occur.

Writing structured objects

Structured objects can also be written out using this same predicate. Thus, given a suitable definition of date_of_birth, the query:

```
?-date_of_birth (shakespeare, D),
    write (D), nl.
```

would produce the answer:

```
date(26, april, 1564)
D = date(26, april, 1564)
```

Lists can also be written out as a single object. Let us define a predicate:

```
writelist (L) :- write (L), nl.
```

This might be used in a query such as:

```
?-writelist ([the, cat, sat, on, the, mat]).

[the, cat, sat, on, the, mat]
yes
```

Since it might look better if the list is written without the square brackets and commas, we can redefine `writelist` to write out each element individually. Each of the elements needs to be separated from its neighbours by a space:

```
writelist ([]) :- nl.
writelist ([Head| Tail]) :- write (Head),
                            write (' '),
                            writelist (Tail).
```

This predicate is useful for writing out more meaningful messages:

```
?-M=january, writelist ([the, month, is, M]).

the month is january
M = january
```

Example: tracing and backtracking

As we have seen, one reason why output does not fit completely naturally into a reasoning-based language like Prolog is that an output cannot be undone once it has taken place. Usually in searching for a solution to a goal, the Prolog system will follow up some paths which eventually prove unfruitful. When this happens, the system will backtrack, undoing decisions it had made earlier. None of this is really visible to the user, who merely sits waiting for the final answer. But now, if the clauses which the system tries to apply include output operations, this output will be displayed whether or not the clauses ultimately prove successful. This may seem to be a nuisance, but it can in fact be quite useful if we actually *want* to know which clauses the system is trying, even if they eventually fail. By arranging for clauses to write out a message each time they are tried, the system can be made to give the appearance of 'thinking aloud'. This gives the ability to *trace* the reasoning process of the system, and to observe the system backtracking as it searches for solutions.

To illustrate this, suppose we wish to trace all uses of the two clauses:

```
likes (mary, X) :- rich (X), handsome (X).
likes (michael, X) :- musical (X), rich (X).
```

To report to the user the fact that the system is trying to apply a particular clause, we should start that clause by writing a message:

```
likes (mary, X) :-
      writelist ([testing, if, mary, likes, X]),
      ...
```

The clause will eventually either succeed or fail, and this answer should also be reported. Reporting success is easy enough: simply include as the very last condition in a clause a condition which will write a message indicating success:

```
likes (mary, X) :-
      ... ,
      writelist ([yes, mary, likes, X]).
```

But what if the clause fails before reaching the end of the clause? The system will not reach this last message-writing predicate, but will instead look for an alternative definition of likes. What we can do, though, is to include a final 'dummy' catch-all likes clause, which will be tried only if all previous attempts fail. If we can arrange for this dummy clause to write out a message reporting failure, and then *fail*, we will have achieved our aim. We need one new Prolog facility to do this neatly.

The 'fail' predicate

How are we going to have to arrange for the dummy predicate above to fail? To force failure, we could write a silly condition such as:

```
5 = 6
```

But this is not very obvious, and it is better to make use of a special built-in Prolog predicate called:

```
fail
```

which always fails.

Using the predicate fail, the last catch-all clause for likes would be written as:

```
likes (X, Y) :-
      writelist ([no, X, does, not, like, Y]),
      fail.
```

With this tracing code included, our two initial clauses have now become:

```
likes (mary, X)  :-
      writelist ([testing, if, mary, likes, X]),
      rich (X),
      handsome (X),
      writelist ([yes, mary, likes, X]).

likes (michael, X)  :-
      writelist ([testing, if, michael, likes, X]),
      musical (X),
      rich (X),
      writelist ([yes, michael, likes, X]).

likes (X, Y)  :-
      writelist ([no, X, does, not, like, Y]),
      fail.
```

If it happens that Michael is indeed rich and handsome, while Mary is musical but not rich, then asking if Mary and Michael like each other using the query:

```
?-likes (mary, michael),
   likes (michael, mary).
```

would produce the response:

```
testing if mary likes michael
yes mary likes michael
testing if michael likes mary
no michael does not like mary
no
```

This ability to observe the system 'thinking aloud' is very useful for correcting a program which is not doing what it is meant to do. This is called *debugging* a program. It is particularly useful for observing the backtracking which the system performs behind the scenes when searching methodically for a solution. Because this facility is so useful, it usually comes built in to the Prolog system, so that it can be used without having to alter your program. Again, the exact details of using this built-in trace (or *spy*) facility will vary depending on which version of Prolog is being used.

5.3   Input in Prolog

Prolog provides a built-in predicate:

```
read  (variable)
```

which succeeds only when the user enters an object on the keyboard.
When evaluating `read`, the system will wait until the user types an object,
and will then set the variable to that object. This way, the user can supply
information to the system during the evaluation of a query.

By way of example, consider a simple program which will accept two
numbers, and output their average. The following predicate will do this:

```
average :- read (N1),
           read (N2),
           Average is (N1 + N2) / 2,
           writelist ([average, is, Average]).
```

A typical interaction might then be:

```
?-average.

21
45
average is 33
yes
```

Prompting the user

If we wish to use the above predicate to find the average of two numbers,
we present the query:

```
?-average.
```

At this point, the system will just sit there, apparently doing nothing. It is
in fact in the middle of:

```
read (N1)
```

waiting for the user to enter the first number. But the user is given no
indication that the next step is up to him or her. This can lead to confusion,
and then frustration. It would make the program much easier to use if at
this point the computer displayed the message:

```
please enter the first number
```

To achieve this, the message must be written before the `read` is attempted.
This has to be programmed, using the `write` predicate, giving us a
revised version of average, as follows:

```
average :-
       writelist ([please, enter,
                   the, first, number]),
```

```
read (N1),
writelist ([please, enter,
            the, second, number]),
read (N2),
Average is (N1 + N2) / 2,
writelist ([average, is, Average]).
```

In general, it is good programming practice always to display a message immediately before doing a read. One purpose of this message is to prompt the user — to let the user know that input is now expected. It is also to give some information on *what* input the user is expected to enter. Small programming points like this are actually quite an important part of giving your programs a friendly user interface.

Example: yes or no answers

Using Prolog's input mechanism, a piece of information which is required to answer a query can often be obtained by asking the user in the middle of answering the query. If this information can be phrased such that the answer needs only to be yes ('y') or no ('n'), we can write a fairly general predicate which will check that the answer actually typed by the user is one of these:

```
answer_yes_or_no (Question, Answer)
```

This predicate asks any supplied question, and returns the answer yes or no. It must first display the supplied question, and read the answer which the user types. If this is either y or n, the predicate should succeed, and set Answer to either yes or no, respectively, in the process. If the user types something other than y or n, then this is an invalid response. In this case the predicate should somehow try again, and only succeed whenever a correct answer has been typed.

The first stages of this predicate are straightforward enough. We assume that the question will be supplied as a list of words. This question will be displayed, and the user's response read. It is also helpful to prompt the user to answer either 'y' or 'n':

```
answer_yes_or_no (Question, Answer) :-
    writelist (Question),
    writelist ([answer, y, or, n]),
    read (Response), nl,
    ...
```

The remainder of the clause must succeed only if the user's typed response is valid: in other words, only if it is y or n. If so, Answer must be set to either yes or no respectively. We will use a separate predicate to define a valid response and its corresponding answer:

```
valid_response (y, yes).
valid_response (n, no).
```

The definition of `answer_yes_or_no` can now be completed:

```
answer_yes_or_no (Question, Answer) :-
    writelist (Question),
    writelist ([answer, y, or, n]),
    read (Response), nl,
    valid_response (Response, Answer).
```

But what if the user types an invalid response (say, an 'm')? If this happens, the condition `valid_response` will fail, and therefore so will our rule for `answer_yes_or_no`. Since we now want the system to ask the question all over again, we merely supply an alternative clause, which will be applied when this first one fails:

```
answer_yes_or_no (Question, Answer) :-
    writelist ([invalid, response]),
    answer_yes_or_no (Question, Answer).
```

This clause will keep on being applied recursively until a valid response is typed. To illustrate the use of this predicate, we might define a predicate:

```
happy (Answer) :-
    answer_yes_or_no ([are, you, happy],
                      Answer).
```

Using this in a query might produce the following interaction:

```
?-happy (Answer).
are you happy
answer y or n
m
invalid response
are you happy
answer y or n
n
Answer = no
```

Querying the user

The predicate `answer_yes_or_no` which we have just developed arrives at a conclusion, not by the usual method of looking up the clauses stored as part of the program, but by asking the user on the spot, interactively. This technique of *querying the user* instead of building all the necessary information into the program is useful, particularly when all the information is not actually *known* when the program is being written. Let us take an example.

In our earlier employment agency program, which contains clauses such as:

```
could_be_trained_as (X, driver) :-
    co_ordinated (X),
    hard_working (X).
```

we have assumed that we have full information about every prospective candidate X. But suppose we want to allow the possibility of a *stranger* appearing on the scene, about whom we obviously have no prior information when writing the program. We would still like to be able to ask:

```
?-could_be_trained_as (stranger, driver).
```

If we ask this query at present, there are no clauses defining the properties of stranger, so this query will fail. However, we can use our technique of querying the user to find the properties of the stranger while the query is being answered. This is done by defining the properties of a special person called stranger as follows:

```
co_ordinated (stranger) :-
    answer_yes_or_no
    ([is, the, stranger, co_ordinated], yes).

hard_working (stranger) :-
    answer_yes_or_no
    ([is, the, stranger, hard_working], yes).

trained_as (stranger, X) :-
    answer_yes_or_no
    ([is, the, stranger, trained, as, a, X],
                                        yes).
...
```

Now if we ask:

```
?-acceptable (hertz, stranger, driver).
```

this could produce the interaction:

```
is the stranger trained as a driver
answer y or n
n
is the stranger co_ordinated
answer y or n
```

```
y
is the stranger hard_working
answer y or n
y
yes
```

5.4   Updating a program in progress

The technique of querying the user for information not originally in the program is a useful technique, but there is a problem. If the information in question is needed at *several* points in the evaluation of a query, then the question will be put to the user every time. This would happen, for instance, in our previous example, where we had the definitions:

```
could_be_trained_as (X, secretary) :-
     accurate (X),
     literate (X),
     outgoing (X).

could_be_trained_as (X, programmer) :-
     clear_thinking (X),
     accurate (X),
     intelligent (X).
```

and the 'query-the-user' properties including:

```
accurate (stranger) :-
     answer_yes_or_no ([is, the, stranger,
                             accurate], yes).
```

If the stranger happens to be accurate, clear-thinking and intelligent, but not literate, then we could well have the following interaction:

```
?-could_be_trained_as (stranger, Skill).

is the stranger accurate
answer y or n
y
is the stranger literate
answer y or n
n
is the stranger clear_thinking
answer y or n
y
is the stranger accurate
answer y  or n
y
```

```
is the stranger intelligent
answer y  or n
y
Skill = programmer
```

Note that the user is asked *twice* if the stranger is accurate. This is because the system does not remember the answer the first time: no record is kept of the answer. What we would really like is, having obtained a yes or no answer, to add this clause to the program immediately, so that it can be used later. Fortunately, Prolog provides built-in facilities which enable clauses to be added to the program, or *asserted*, during the process of answering a query. These clauses are then used as though they were part of the original program.

Rather than providing just a single built-in predicate which asserts a clause, Prolog gives a little extra control over where the clause is to be inserted in the program. Since there may already be several existing definitions of the relationship being asserted, we have the option of placing the new clause either at the *start* of the existing definitions, or at the *end*. Prolog therefore provides two built-in predicates. One is:

```
asserta (clause)
```

This asserts the given clause at the start of any existing definitions of the relationship being defined. The other predicate is:

```
assertz (clause)
```

This asserts the given clause at the end of any existing definitions of the relationship being defined. The final letters in these predicate names ('a' and 'z'), being the first and last letters of the alphabet, have been chosen to help you remember where the new clause goes. In each case, the predicate will succeed, and assert the new clause as a side-effect. Note that, just like output in Prolog, the effects of these predicates cannot be undone by backtracking. If a clause is asserted while evaluating a query, it will not somehow disappear just because the query fails.

Now consider how these facilities can be used to prevent the program repeatedly querying the user for the same piece of information. Take the case, for instance, where we want to avoid asking twice if the stranger is accurate. The main action which needs to be taken is to record the answer which the user gives the first time the information is required. This is done by asserting the answer as a fact:

```
known_to_be_accurate (stranger, Answer).
```

Thus, to determine if the stranger is accurate, the program should *first* look to see if the answer has previously been recorded; only as a last resort should the user be queried. This ordering can be achieved by having a final user-querying definition of known_to_be_accurate, and arranging for the user's answer to be asserted *before* this definition. Thus, the original program will just have the single definition:

```
known_to_be_accurate (Person, Answer) :-
    answer_yes_or_no
            ([is, Person, accurate], Answer),
    asserta (known_to_be_accurate
                        (Person, Answer)).
```

The first time the program applies this clause, the user will be queried, and a new clause asserted. Supposing the user answered 'y', then the program would at this point contain two definitions for the predicate:

```
known_to_be_accurate (stranger, no).
known_to_be_accurate (Person, Answer) :-
    answer_yes_or_no
            ([is, Person, accurate], Answer),
    asserta (known_to_be_accurate
                        (Person, Answer)).
```

Finally, to define the conditions under which the stranger is in fact accurate, this property can be redefined by the clause:

```
accurate (Person) :-
    known_to_be_accurate (Person, Answer),
    Answer = yes.
```

In actual fact, this formulation of accurate is not confined to just stranger: it could be used for any candidate. Testing if any person was accurate would result in a query to the user, and the answer would then be recorded in the program. Using this approach for each property in the program, the program need not initially contain the properties of *anyone*. Then, as the program is used, these properties will gradually be defined as facts, using the answers supplied by the user. This approach therefore has the potential to make programs less specific, and able to 'grow' in knowledge. In a very simplistic way, a program is now able to learn.

Retracting clauses

Just as we might want to update the stored database of clauses by asserting new clauses, so too there are times when we want to state that an old clause is out of date, and should be retracted, or deleted from the program. Prolog provides a facility for this, using the built-in predicate:

```
retract (clause)
```

The predicate `retract` will go through the program, looking for a clause which matches the supplied one. If it finds a matching clause, it will remove it from the program. This is particularly useful for modifying program clauses which define things which change with time. A simple example might be today's date. If a program needed to know today's date, then it would be useful to have today's date defined as a clause. This is often needed, for instance, to work out how long ago certain historical events took place:

```
todays_date (date(1, february, 1988)).
```

Obviously, though, this 'fact' will be out of date in twenty-four hours time. The next day, when the program is used, what we should do is retract this definition, and assert the new date. A simple predicate which does this might be:

```
set_new_date :- todays_date (Old),
        writelist ([old, date, is, D]),
        writelist ([enter, new, date]),
        read (New),
        retract (todays_date (Old)),
        asserta (todays_date (New)).
```

If you have ever used another programming language which has the concept of *assignment*, then this is how it is done in Prolog. The old value must be retracted, and the new one asserted. Except for certain simple cases like the one above, it is not to be recommended!

EXERCISES

1 A game of buzz

Try counting out loud from 1 up to 100, but replace every number which is divisible by either three or seven with the word *buzz*. This should give a sequence starting as follows:

1 2 *buzz* 4 5 *buzz* *buzz* 8 *buzz* 10 11 ...

Write a Prolog program which will display the correct sequence (up to 100) on the screen.

2 Formatting list output

The predicate `writelist` given earlier in the chapter becomes rather unsatisfactory when the supplied list has a large number of elements. The problem is that the display overshoots the end of the line. In these situations, to control exactly when a new line is taken, we might wish to write the list, say, four elements per line. Write a general predicate:

```
format_list (List, Width)
```

which writes out the supplied list with Width elements on every line, except possibly the last. For instance, the query:

```
?-format_list ([1, 2, 3, 4, 5,
                6, 7, 8, 9, 10], 4).
```

should display the list in the format:

```
1    2    3    4
5    6    7    8
9    10
yes
```

3 Setting the time

In section 5.4, we met a predicate:

```
set_new_date
```

which queried the user for the current date, and then updated the program dynamically to define this date as todays_date. We wish to do the same for defining the current time.

The current time will be defined in the program by a predicate:

```
time_now (time)
```

The value returned by this predicate as the current time has now to be redefined by writing a predicate:

```
set_new_time
```

This predicate should do several things:

(i) Display the time now, as defined at present in the program.
(ii) Accept the new time from the user.
(iii) *Check* the supplied input time, and re-input it if it was invalid (see later).
(iv) Update the program by redefining the predicate time_now.

Assuming a twenty-four hour time system, a time could be represented by the Prolog object:

```
time(hours, minutes, seconds)
```

An invalid time could be something like:

```
time(25, 99, 99)
```

You will need to write a predicate:

```
valid_time (T)
```

which succeeds only if T is a valid time object. This must check each of the three components of a *time* object, to see that each is in the appropriate range.

Try to make the operation of the predicate set_time_now as user-friendly as possible.

PART TWO

Applications of Prolog

6

An application in
language translation

Language translation is a booming business in Europe at present, thanks
largely to the European Economic Community. Because of its bureaucratic
and multilingual nature, large numbers of documents have to be translated
into many different languages. For instance, at the last count, a document
written in English which has to be circulated around the EEC must first be
translated into eight other languages. This sort of translation work tends to
be exceedingly boring and tedious, so it seems an obvious candidate for
computerisation.

We will consider how to go about the task of translation, beginning
with the simplest approach of word-for-word translation. The
shortcomings of this simplistic approach will soon become obvious, and
we will then progress to a slightly better technique. This will lead
eventually to a Prolog program for translating a very restricted class of
sentence between English and French. Of course, this treatment has to be
very superficial, since the difficulty of doing real translation is enormous.
So do not assume that progressing to a larger class of sentence will just be
a matter of extending the final program a bit. Nevertheless, many of the
basic techniques of language processing can be picked up by considering
this problem.

6.1 Word-for-word translation

A recent advertisement for a hand-held device (looking suspiciously like a
calculator) promises:

> *Speak a foreign language in seconds!*
> *The world's first pocket-sized translator*

109

At $53.95, could this solve the EEC's translation problems? Actually, the device is merely a small dictionary, with 4000 English words and their equivalent in another language. It is easy to write a simple Prolog program to do the same thing, as we will now see.

A Prolog dictionary

The English meaning of a French word can be defined using a predicate:

    means (*French word, English word*)

For instance, a very small French/English vocabulary could be defined as follows:

```
means (chat, cat).
means (est, is).
means (le, the).
means (la, the).
means (tapis, mat).
means (sur, on).
```

These definitions can be used to translate individual words, as illustrated by the following queries:

(i) *What is the French for 'cat'?* This is found by presenting the Prolog query:

```
?-means (French, mat).
```

which produces the answer:

```
French = tapis
```

(ii) *What is the French for 'the'?* In Prolog:

```
?-means (French, the).
```

Note that there is more than one answer to this:

```
French = le;
French = la;
no
```

(iii) *What is the English for 'le chat'?* In Prolog:

```
?-means (le, Word1), means (chat, Word2).
```

which produces the answer:

```
Word1 = the
Word2 = cat
```

Note that the predicate means can be used to translate in either direction. Thus already we have a two-way dictionary, defining a small vocabulary. The only limitation is how many words the computer can hold. We will now use this Prolog dictionary to do a simple word for word translation of a whole sentence.

Translating sentences

A sentence can be represented in Prolog as a list of words. For instance, the English sentence:

The cat sat on the mat

would be held as the Prolog list:

```
[the, cat, sat, on, the, mat]
```

Likewise, the French sentence:

Pierre est sur le tapis

could be held in Prolog as:

```
[pierre, est, sur, le, tapis]
```

Translating a list of words from French to English is just a list processing operation. We require a predicate:

```
translate ([...French words...], [...English words...])
```

This predicate will be tackled in the usual list processing way. The supplied list of French words can be either empty or non-empty. To translate an empty list of French words is straightforward:

```
translate ([], []).
```

For the non-empty case, the list of French words is treated as an initial word (the head) followed by the list of remaining words (the tail). The resulting list of English words will have the same structure. The tail is translated by using translate recursively:

```
translate ([F_head| F_tail],
           [E_head| E_tail]) :-
     means (F_head, E_head),
     translate (F_tail, E_tail).
```

The following examples illustrate the use of this predicate.

(i) To translate the sentence:

Le chat est sur le tapis

present the query:

```
?-translate ([le, chat, est, sur, le, tapis],
                English).
```

This would produce the answer:

```
English = [the, cat, is, on, the, mat]
```

(ii) We can use the same predicate to translate in the other direction, from English into French. Given a larger vocabulary, the query:

```
?-translate (French, [peter, eats, the, cat]).
```

would produce the answer:

```
French = [pierre, mange, le, chat]
```

Note in passing the way Prolog predicates such as `means` and `translate` can be used in two directions. We can supply either of the two arguments, and obtain the other as the answer. This reversible nature of Prolog predicates is important, and very useful. We will make considerable use of it later on.

The predicate `translate` seems to give quite impressive results for such a simple program. But very soon its limitations show up.

Problem 1: *word order*

Suppose you happen to be visiting a French friend in Paris on a rainy day. His cats have just come in dripping wet, and settle themselves on the mat in front of the fire. Your friend points to his cats and says:

Voici les chats mouilles sur le tapis!

meaning, of course:

See the wet cats on the mat!

However, if you use the above Prolog program to translate this sentence, you would suddenly become very wary of the cats (not to mention the mat):

```
?-translate ([voici, les, chats, mouilles,
              sur, le, tapis], English).

English = [see, the, cats, wet, on, the, mat]
```

The problem is with adjectives in French. An adjective is a word which describes something, like `mouilles` in this case. In French, an adjective comes *after* the noun it is describing, whereas in English an adjective comes *before* the noun. Clearly, then, we will have to consider word order when translating a sentence. Word order is an important ingredient in giving the meaning of a sentence. Consider, for instance:

on cat black the mat the is

This is meaningless because the words are not in any expected order. There are rules which specify what order the words have to be in for it to be a proper sentence. The expected order of the words in the above sentence is presumably:

the black cat	is	on	the mat
noun phrase	*verb*	*preposition*	*noun phrase*

Note that to check the word order, we have to analyse the *structure* of the sentence; this involves dividing the sentence up into its different sections (or phrases). Valid word order in English is specified by the rules of normal English grammar. A *grammar* is used to work out the structure of the sentence, and to break it up into its various components (noun phrase, verb, and so on). Words appear in a different order in French because French grammar is different from English grammar. To get the word order right, we will have to work out the structure of a sentence before translating it. Splitting up a sentence into its different parts, and analysing its structure, is called *parsing*.

Problem 2: *ambiguities*

When translating the article 'the' into French, there are several possible translations. These include 'le' and 'la'. One reason for there being different possible French translations of the same English word is that French words have *gender*, whereas English words rarely do. By gender we mean whether a thing is *masculine* or *feminine*. The word 'le' is used when talking of something which is masculine, while 'la' is used for things feminine. Thus, the right choice depends on what 'the' applies to. So a word-for-word translation approach breaks down here. Again, we will need to detect the structure of the sentence to see what the various parts refer to. The rules for matching the article ('le', 'la', and so forth) with what it refers to are again part of French grammar.

Problem 3: *bad grammar*

Our program so far would happily accept a sentence like:

the cats is on the mat

where the subject is plural but the verb is singular. The individual words themselves are valid, and the order is right, but when put together the sentence is not. This is because the *number* of the subject (either singular or plural) and the number of the verb are not the same in this case: *cats* is plural, while *is* is singular. Yet again, the rules for what is allowable in this context are part of English grammar.

Problem 4: *understanding*

Often in translation it is necessary to understand what is being said before a proper translation can be made. The problem of understanding a sentence goes far beyond checking word order and other grammatical rules. Even if the word order in a sentence is perfect, even if all the rules of grammar are obeyed, the sentence may still not make sense. For instance:

The banana galloped the octopus

Analysing the meaning of a sentence is an extremely difficult problem. In fact, we will ignore it totally throughout the remainder of this chapter. Instead, we will confine our approach to analysing the structure and other grammatical aspects.

To tackle the first three problems above, we will have to get beyond a crude word-for-word approach to translation. To make any headway, we have got to be able to analyse the structure of a sentence — to parse it. To do this will first require a simple English grammar to be defined.

6.2   A grammar for simple English

We can define the structure of simple English sentences by a few rules. For instance, the sentence:

the   dog   bit   the   man

has the structure:

noun phrase + *verb* + *noun phrase*

But this general structure would not necessarily apply to cases such as:

the   dog   barked

which have the structure:

noun phrase + *verb*

But neither of these alternative definitions of a sentence is sufficient for:

the black cat	is	on	the mat
noun phrase +	*verb* +	*preposition* +	*noun phrase*

After some further thought, we might eventually come up with the following set of rules, which specify the structure of a subset of simple English sentences:

> *sentence*   =   *noun_phrase verb_phrase*

{ There are three different allowable forms of noun_phrase: }

> *noun_phrase*   =   *article adjective noun*
> > {e.g. 'the black cat'   }
>
> *noun_phrase*   =   *article noun*
> > {e.g. 'the mat'   }
>
> *noun_phrase*   =   *name*
> > {e.g. 'Peter'   }

{ There are two different allowable forms of verb_phrase: }

> *verb_phrase*   =   *verb prep_phrase*
> > {e.g. 'is on the mat'   }
>
> *verb_phrase*   =   *verb*
> > {e.g. 'barks'   }

{ There are two different allowable forms of prep_phrase: }

> *prep_phrase*   =   *preposition noun_phrase*
> > {e.g. 'on the mat'   }
>
> *prep_phrase*   =   *noun_phrase*

This defines the general structure and word order of simple English sentences. The first rule, for instance, states that a sentence is valid if it consists of a noun phrase followed by a verb phrase. This part of a grammar is called the *syntax*. The other part is the *vocabulary*, which defines the valid basic words. A word can be either a noun, a verb, an article, an adjective, a name or a preposition. For instance, to indicate that the word *cat* is a noun, we could use the same notation and write:

> *noun*   =   *cat*

Other definitions in the vocabulary might be:

> *article*   =   *the*
> *article*   =   *a*
> *noun*   =   *mat*

verb	=	*is*
verb	=	*kicked*
verb	=	*barked*
adjective	=	*black*
name	=	*Peter*
preposition	=	*on*

...

Note that we could add many more words to this vocabulary, without having to change the rules for the syntax.

The above syntax rules and vocabulary together give us a grammar. Using this grammar (and an extended vocabulary), we can now parse sentences by hand. This involves identifying the different structures or components within the sentence, and grouping the individual words into the phrases defined in the grammar. For instance, consider the sentence:

> *the black cat is on the mat*

Assuming this to be a sentence, we know from the grammar that we expect there to be two components in the sentence: a noun phrase, and a verb phrase. Noticing that the first definition of a noun phrase matches the first three words of the sentence, and recognising that the last four words constitute a valid verb phrase, we can draw out the structure of the sentence in the following way:

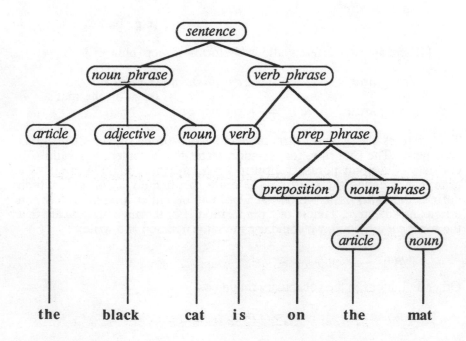

Note that the structure of the sentence can be represented in this way by what is called a *tree* (often called a *structure tree*, or in this context, a *parse tree*). Turning the diagram upside down perhaps gives a hint as to why this term is used. The very top object, or *node* (which in the above tree is *sentence*) is called the *root* of the tree. Many objects with structure can be represented by a tree.

Another example, this time of a simpler sentence, is:

> *Peter   barked*

which has the structure tree:

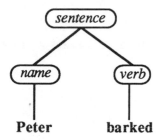

Note though that, according to the above grammar:

> *Peter kicked the cat on the mat*

is not a simple English sentence. There is no way that the words of this sentence can be made to fit into the phrase structure defined by the simple grammar we are using. An attempt to do so would probably get as far as the first four words:

> *Peter kicked the cat*

and then discover that there were still some words left which had no counterpart in the grammar.

The parsing process, whereby the different parts of a sentence are recognised, is not a trivial process. But it is fundamental to processing the sentence in any meaningful way, since any useful processing requires knowledge of the structure of the sentence. We will therefore develop a Prolog program which parses simple English sentences automatically. But first, consider the simple task of representing the vocabulary in Prolog.

A vocabulary in Prolog

A vocabulary gives information about what sort of word each item in the vocabulary is: whether it is a noun, or a verb, or a preposition, or whatever. The fact that a word such as *mat* is a noun can be defined in Prolog by the predicate:

```
noun (mat).
```

In general, a predicate is required for each class of word; this gives the following set of predicates for our simple grammar:

```
article       (Word).
noun          (Word).
name          (Word).
adjective     (Word).
verb          (Word).
preposition   (Word).
```

A simple vocabulary is just a collection of facts defined using these predicates. For instance:

```
article       (a).
article       (the).
noun          (cat).
noun          (mat).
name          (fred).
name          (peter).
adjective     (black).
adjective     (furry).
adjective     (wet).
verb          (is).
verb          (barked).
preposition   (on).
...
```

If a word has two meanings (such as *fish*, which we might wish to regard either as an noun or a verb), then there should be a definition for each possible meaning:

```
noun          (fish).
verb          (fish).
```

These predicates will be used to check the structure of groups of words. For instance, to test that the phrase:

the black cat

has the structure:

article adjective noun

we could use the query:

```
?-article (the),
  adjective (black),
  noun (cat).
```

This facility will be used extensively when parsing a sentence, and trying to recognise its structure.

6.3   A Prolog parser for English sentences

We want a predicate which succeeds if a sentence can be parsed properly, and fails if it cannot. So if this predicate is applied to the sentence:

> *Peter kicked the cat on the mat*

then it should fail, since this sentence cannot be parsed according to our simple grammar.

Consider the problem of checking that a list of words is a valid sentence, and recall that a sentence will be held as a Prolog list. A list of words is a valid sentence if:

- the list has a valid noun phrase at the front;
- what is left after the noun phrase is a valid verb phrase.

Therefore, given the list of words:

the	black	cat	is	on	the	mat

the first question which needs to be asked is:

> *Does this list have a valid noun phrase at the front?*
> *If so, remove the noun phrase from the list.*

The answer to this question will turn out to be yes, and removing the noun phrase from the front leaves the list:

is	on	the	mat

The question to be asked at this point is:

> *Does this list have a valid verb phrase at the front?*
> *If so, remove the verb phrase from the list.*

Again, the answer to this turns out to be yes; removing the verb phrase from the list leaves just the empty list.

This illustrates the general strategy for parsing a list of words:

- Take the input list.
- Identify each of the expected components or phrases, one at a time.
- Each time a phrase is identified, remove it from the front of the list.
- This remainder is used as the list for identifying the next component.
- At the very end, there will be a remainder list (possibly empty); this will be returned by the process as a left-over.

Parsing a sentence is just a special case of parsing any type of phrase or structure. Therefore, for each sort of structure (a sentence, a noun phrase, or whatever) we will have a separate predicate. Each predicate will take an input list, and will specify the conditions under which there is an occurrence of that structure at the front of the list. If the predicate succeeds, it will return the left-over as an output list; this will be what is left of the input list after the structure has been stripped off the front. If the input list does not meet the conditions, the predicate should fail.

Sentences

Consider first the predicate which defines what a valid sentence is. As with any predicate which parses a structure, there will be an input list and an output (remainder) list:

```
sentence ([...input list...], [...output list...]) :- ...
```

In completing this predicate, we will assume the existence of whatever other predicates are required. (If they do not exist, they can be written later.) The actual predicate is:

```
sentence (In, Out) :-
      noun_phrase (In, Temp),
      verb_phrase (Temp, Out).
```

This states that the input list In has a valid sentence at the front (returning a left-over list of words called Out) if In starts with a noun phrase (leaving an intermediate, or temporary list Temp) and Temp starts with a verb phrase (leaving the remainder list Out). Diagrammatically, the division of the list is as follows:

Assuming that the predicates noun_phrase and verb_phrase have been defined, we could now ask:

```
?-sentence
    ([the, black, cat, is, on, the, mat], []).
```

This would return the answer ye s. Note that the query specifies that the remainder list must be empty. The query:

```
?-sentence ([peter, ate, the, cat,
                on, the, mat], Out).
```

would actually succeed, returning the answer:

```
Out = [on, the, mat]
```

This is because the noun phrase (peter) and the verb phrase (ate the cat) are both stripped off, leaving the remainder as shown.

Noun phrases

Now consider the definition of noun_phrase:

```
noun_phrase  ([...input list...],  [...output list...])
```

So far, it has just been assumed that this predicate will do its job, but now it must be defined in full. According to our grammar, there are three possible forms a valid noun phrase can take, so we will have three separate Prolog clauses, each of which will define one valid form of a noun_phrase.

1st case: *noun_phrase = article adjective noun*

The detailed format of the input list of words which has a noun phrase of this sort at the front (and which has a left-over list of words called Out) is as follows:

The predicate which checks that the input list conforms to this pattern is:

```
noun_phrase ([Art, Adj, Nn| Out], Out)  :-
    article (Art),
    adjective (Adj),
    noun (Nn).
```

This predicate takes an input list of words and decomposes it; the first word is called `Art`, the second `Adj`, the third `Nn`, and the remaining list of words is called `Out`. Note that it is by placing this same remainder list in the output position that we strip off the noun phrase from the input list. Next, the first three words are tested to check that they are of the right class. If the decomposition and the checks all succeed, then the predicate succeeds. For instance, the query:

```
?-noun_phrase ([the, fat, man, dozed], Out).
```

would succeed, setting `Out` to the list `[dozed]`, whereas the query:

```
?-noun_phrase ([the, fat, lazy, man, dozed], Out).
```

would fail at the third condition in `noun_phrase`, where the third word in the list (referred to within the predicate as `Nn`) is being tested by the predicate `noun`. The condition:

```
noun (lazy)
```

would fail, assuming that `lazy` had been defined as an adjective.

2nd case: *noun_phrase = article noun*

The detailed format of an input list which has a noun phrase of this second type at its front is:

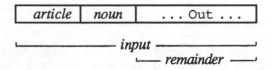

A second definition of the predicate `noun_phrase` which succeeds only if the input list has this structure is as follows:

```
noun_phrase ([Art, Nn| Out], Out) :-
    article (Art),
    noun (Nn).
```

3rd case: *noun_phrase = name*

In this case, the input list must merely start with a word which has been defined to be a name. Everything after this word in the list is the remainder. The predicate is therefore:

```
noun_phrase ([Name| Out], Out) :-
    name (Name).
```

The following example queries illustrate the operation of noun_phrase:

(i)   ?-noun_phrase ([peter, barked], [barked]).

This succeeds; the first two definitions of noun_phrase are tried, and fail. But the third clause matches.

(ii)   ?-noun_phrase ([the, black, cat, is,
                        on, the, mat], Out).

The first clause defining noun_phrase successfully parses this input list, and produces the answer:

    Out = [is, on, the, mat]

(iii)   ?-noun_phrase ([on, the, mat], Out).

This will fail; none of the three clauses for noun_phrase will match this input list.

Verb phrases

A valid verb phrase can be defined by two alternative clauses for a predicate verb_phrase. This predicate should succeed if the input list of words begins with a valid verb phrase, in which case the list of remaining words should be returned as the output list:

    verb_phrase ([...*input list*...], [...*output list*...])

Again, consider each of the two cases of a verb phrase as defined in the grammar separately.

1st case: *verb_phrase = verb prep_phrase*

For the input list of words to start with a verb phrase of this particular form, it must have the following structure:

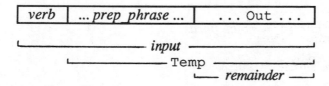

An input list which has this structure is defined by the predicate:

```
verb_phrase ([V| Temp], Out) :-
        verb (V),
        prep_phrase (Temp, Out).
```

This states that an input list of words is a valid verb phrase of this type if the first word is a verb, and if what comes after this verb (the list `Temp`) starts with a preposition phrase. The left-over from `prep_phrase` is then the left-over from the whole verb phrase.

2nd case: *verb_phrase = verb*

The clause which defines this alternative succeeds if the first word is a verb, and returns the input list of words minus this first word:

```
verb_phrase ([V| Out], Out) :-
    verb (V).
```

For example, the query:

```
?-verb_phrase ([is, on, the, mat], Out).
```

will succeed. The first clause is selected, setting `Out` to the empty list. Likewise, the query:

```
?-verb_phrase ([barked], []).
```

will succeed.

Preposition phrases

The grammar states that there are two forms which a valid preposition phrase can take. We will consider each case separately, and define a clause for each one.

1st case: *prep_phrase = preposition noun_phrase*

An input list of words which has this structure is defined by the predicate:

```
prep_phrase ([Prep| Temp], Out) :-
    preposition (Prep),
    noun_phrase (Temp, Out).
```

2nd case: *prep_phrase = noun_phrase*

This case is defined by:

```
prep_phrase (In, Out) :-
    noun_phrase (In, Out).
```

For example, the following query will succeed:

```
?-prep_phrase ([on, the, furry, mat], []).
```

The first clause for `prep_phrase` will be selected to parse this input list of words.

The complete parsing program

Gathering together all the predicates defined so far, plus the vocabulary definitions, gives a complete program which checks for proper structure of simple English sentences, as shown below. This program is fundamental to any language processing, and should be thoroughly understood. We will call it Program 1.

```
sentence (In, Out)  :-
    noun_phrase (In, Temp),
    verb_phrase (Temp, Out).


noun_phrase ([Art, Adj, Nn| Out], Out)  :-
    article (Art),
    adjective (Adj),
    noun (Nn).

noun_phrase ([Art, Nn| Out], Out)  :-
    article (Art),
    noun (Nn).

noun_phrase ([Name| Out], Out)  :-
    name (Name).


verb_phrase ([V| Temp], Out)  :-
    verb (V),
    prep_phrase (Temp, Out).

verb_phrase ([V| Out], Out)  :-
    verb (V).

prep_phrase ([Prep| Temp], Out)  :-
    preposition (Prep),
    noun_phrase (Temp, Out).

prep_phrase (In, Out)  :-
    noun_phrase (In, Out).


article        (a).
article        (the).
noun           (cat).
noun           (mat).
```

```
name              (fred).
name              (peter).
adjective         (black).
adjective         (furry).
adjective         (wet).
verb              (is).
verb              (barked).
preposition       (on).
```

Program 1 *A Prolog parser for simple English sentences*

Example trace

Let us trace the evaluation of the goal:

```
sentence ([peter, eats, the, black, cat], Out)?

    noun_phrase ([peter, eats, the,
                            black, cat], Temp) ?

        { Try first clause for noun_phrase }
        article (peter) ?
        - fails

        { Try second clause for noun_phrase }
        article (peter) ?
        - fails

        { Try final clause for noun_phrase }
        name (peter) ?
        - succeeds

    - succeeds, setting Temp to [eats,the,black,cat]

    verb_phrase ([eats, the, black, cat],
                                    Out) ?

        { Try the first clause for verb_phrase:      }
        { initially sets                             }
        { V = eats, Temp = [the, black, cat]         }

        verb (eats) ?
        - succeeds

        prep_phrase ([the, black, cat], Out) ?

            { Try the first clause for prep_phrase: }
```

```
preposition (the) ?
- fails
```

{ Try the second clause for prep_phrase }
```
noun_phrase ([the, black, cat],
                            Out) ?
```

{ Try the first clause for   }
{ noun_phrase: }
{ initially sets Out = []   }

```
article (the) ?
- succeeds
adjective (black) ?
- succeeds
noun (cat) ?
- succeeds
```

- *succeeds*, returning output list [ ]

- *succeeds*, returning output list [ ]

- *succeeds*, returning output list [ ]

- *succeeds*, returning output list [ ]

6.4   Checking other grammatical points

Our simple grammar defines only the structure of valid sentences. But structure is not the only feature of good grammar. Consider, for instance, the following sentence which conforms to our grammar:

the   cats   is on the mat

noun phrase   *verb phrase*

Our grammar at present allows sentences to succeed where singulars and plurals do not match up. We will now extend the grammar so that it specifies the number (singular or plural) of words and structures.

Adding number to the vocabulary

First, we have to extend the definition of basic words in the vocabulary to say whether they are singular or plural. The number of a verb is the number of the subject of the verb; for instance, *eats* is singular, since we cannot say that *cats eats*. Likewise with the number of an article. Adjectives are the same whether they are describing something singular or something plural, so they have no associated number. Similarly, prepositions have no associated number. Some words are definitely singular, such as *cat*, or *is* or *a*; others are definitely plural, such as *mats* or *are*. But some can be thought of as either singular or plural, such as *the*, which can refer either to something singular like *cat*, or to something plural like *cats*. To handle this in Prolog, we will give a separate definition for each case. To indicate the number of a word, the defining predicate is extended where appropriate, as shown below. Singular is denoted by *s*, and plural by *p*.

```
article        (the,     s).
article        (the,     p).
article        (a,       s).
noun           (cat,     s).
noun           (cats,    p).
noun           (mat,     s).
noun           (mats,    p).
name           (fred,    s).
name           (peter,   s).
adjective      (black).
adjective      (furry).
adjective      (wet).
verb           (is,      s).
verb           (are,     p).
verb           (barked,  s).
verb           (barked,  p).
preposition    (on).
```

Adding number to clauses

We now have to extend the Prolog clauses in the parser program to do the matching of singulars and plurals as it goes along. Consider, for instance, the rules for a sentence:

> *a singular noun phrase requires a singular verb phrase*
> *a plural noun phrase requires a plural verb phrase*

Clearly, we will need to know the number of a complete phrase such as a `noun_phrase` or a `verb_phrase` before we can check these rules. To obtain this, the rules for these components will have to be extended, just as we extended the vocabulary rules to include the number. (The difference is that with a basic word the number could be looked up, whereas for a phrase it has to be worked out.) Again, we will work through each structure in turn.

Noun phrases

Since a complete noun phrase can itself be either singular or plural, the predicate for a noun phrase should be extended to define the number of the noun phrase:

```
noun_phrase (input list, output list, number) :- ...
```

The number of the noun phrase will be denoted by s if the noun phrase is singular, and p if it is plural. For instance:

```
?-noun_phrase ([peter], [], s).
```

should succeed;

```
?-noun_phrase ([a, cat], [], p).
```

should fail;

```
?-noun_phrase ([the, cats], [], N).
```

should succeed, and set N to p.

Now consider each of the three different forms of noun phrase as defined by the grammar.

1st case: *noun_phrase = article adjective noun*

The rule for singular and plural in this case is that the number of the article and the number of the noun must be the same. The adjective, which has no associated number, has no bearing on the matter. The number of the overall noun phrase is then the number of the article and noun. These conditions can be defined quite easily in Prolog, by extending the previous Prolog clause for this case as follows:

```
noun_phrase ([Art, Adj, Nn| Out], Out,
                                    Number) :-
        article (Art, N),
        adjective (Adj),
        noun (Nn, N).
```

Note the use of the same variable name N in the number position of both article and noun; it is this which causes failure if the number of each is not the same. For instance, in the query:

```
?-noun_phrase ([a, black, cats], Out, N).
```

the first condition sets N to s; but the predicate will then fail on the last condition:

```
noun (cats, s)
```

2nd case: *noun_phrase = article noun*

The rule in this case is that the number of the article and the noun must agree. This can be defined by a similar extension to the earlier clause for this case:

```
noun_phrase ([Art, Nn| Out], Out, N) :-
    article (Art, N),
    noun (Nn, N).
```

3rd case: *noun_phrase = name*

All that has to be done in this case is to return the number of the name (picked up from the vocabulary) as the number of the entire noun phrase:

```
noun_phrase ([Name| Out], Out, N) :-
    name (Name, N).
```

For instance, the query:

```
?-noun_phrase ([peter, barked], Out, N).
```

will succeed, producing the answer:

```
Out = [barked]
N = s
```

Verb phrases

Again, the two clauses for verb_phrase will need to be extended, both to check the internal number agreement of the verb phrase, and also to return the number of the phrase as a whole. For instance, the phrase:

   sits on the mats

is singular because the vocabulary states that the verb *sits* is singular. Note that there is no need for agreement between the verb and the rest of the phrase.

1st case: *verb_phrase = verb prep_phrase*

Since there is no need for any agreement between the verb and the preposition phrase, all that this predicate has to do is to return the number of the verb as the number of the whole verb phrase. In fact, there is no need to associate a number with a preposition phrase at all, since it never has to agree with anything. This gives the following definition of verb_phrase for this case:

```
verb_phrase ([V| Temp], Out, N) :-
    verb (V, N),
    prep_phrase (Temp, Out).
```

2nd case: *verb_phrase = verb*

The clause for this case has merely to return the number of the verb as the number of the verb phrase:

```
verb_phrase ([V| Out], Out, N) :-
    verb (V, N).
```

Preposition phrases

We have seen already that there are no number agreement rules especially for preposition phrases. It makes no difference whether a cat sits *on the mat* or *on the mats*. This will make things rather simple.

1st case: *prep_phrase = preposition noun_phrase*

The new version of noun_phrase will still return the number of the noun phrase, whether we intend to use it or not. In this context, it is safe to ignore the number of the noun phrase:

```
prep_phrase ([Prep| Temp], Out) :-
    preposition (Prep),
    noun_phrase (Temp, Out, _).
```

2nd case: *prep_phrase = noun_phrase*

Again, the number of the noun phrase can be ignored:

```
prep_phrase (In, Out) :-
    noun_phrase (In, Out, _).
```

Sentences

Finally, let us return to the predicate which defines the number agreement between the two components of a sentence: the noun phrase and the verb phrase. The number of each part has to be the same. However, there is no need to associate a number with a sentence. This gives us the following predicate which defines the necessary number agreement for a sentence:

```
sentence (In, Out) :-
     noun_phrase (In, Temp, N),
     verb_phrase (Temp, Out, N).
```

For instance, given the query:

```
?-sentence ([the, cat, are, on, the, mat], []).
```

noun_phrase will set N to s, but verb_phrase will then fail. It will actually fail when trying:

```
verb (are, s)
```

The complete number-checking program

Gathering together all the extended definitions in this new section gives the following program, which not only parses an input list of words, but also checks for number agreement throughout the sentence. This is Program 2.

```
sentence (In, Out) :-
     noun_phrase (In, Temp, N),
     verb_phrase (Temp, Out, N).


noun_phrase ([Art, Adj, Nn| Out], Out,
                                     Number):-
     article (Art, N),
     adjective (Adj),
     noun (Nn,  N).

noun_phrase ([Art, Nn| Out], Out, N) :-
     article (Art, N),
     noun (Nn, N).

noun_phrase ([Name| Out], Out, N) :-
     name (Name, N).


verb_phrase ([V| Temp], Out, N) :-
     verb (V, N),
     prep_phrase (Temp, Out).

verb_phrase ([V| Out], Out, N) :-
     verb (V, N).

prep_phrase ([Prep| Temp], Out) :-
     preposition (Prep),
     noun_phrase (Temp, Out, _).
```

```
prep_phrase (In, Out) :-
     noun_phrase (In, Out, _).

article          (the,    s).
article          (the,    p).
article          (a,      s).
noun             (cat,    s).
noun             (cats,   p).
noun             (mat,    s).
noun             (mats,   p).
name             (fred,   s).
name             (peter,  s).
adjective        (black).
adjective        (furry).
adjective        (wet).
verb             (is,     s).
verb             (are,    p).
verb             (barked, s).
verb             (barked, p).
preposition      (on).
```

Program 2 *A parser and checker for simple English sentences*

6.5   A parser for simple French sentences

Simple sentences in French sometimes have a similar structure to English sentences. For our simple French language, the only significant difference will be in noun phrases, where an adjective comes *after* the noun it describes, rather than before it. For instance, to describe a black cat in French we would say:

> le   chat   noir
>
> *article   noun   adjective*

Apart from this, a grammar defining simple French sentences will be very similar to our earlier grammar for English sentences. An actual grammar for simple French sentences is given below. To avoid confusion between a structure in English grammar and in French grammar, French structures will have their name prefixed with an 'f_'.

f_sentence	= *f_noun_phrase f_verb_phrase*
f_noun_phrase	= *f_article f_noun f_adjective*
f_noun_phrase	= *f_article f_noun*
f_noun_phrase	= *f_name*
f_verb_phrase	= *f_verb f_prep_phrase*
f_verb_phrase	= *f_verb*

> *f_prep_phrase*   = *f_preposition f_noun_phrase*
> *f_prep_phrase*   = *f_noun_phrase*

A Prolog French vocabulary

A French vocabulary will of course be different from an English one, but it is defined in the same way. Writing the vocabulary as Prolog facts might give the following simple vocabulary:

```
f_article        (un).
f_article        (une).
f_article        (le).
f_article        (la).
f_article        (les).
f_noun           (chat).
f_noun           (chats).
f_name           (pierre).
f_verb           (est).
f_verb           (sont).
f_adjective      (noir).
f_adjective      (noire).
f_preposition    (sur).
...
```

A Prolog parser for French sentences

Since any parsing program follows naturally from the grammar, a parsing program for simple French sentences will obviously be very similar to our English parser. In fact, apart from making the predicate names different (by putting an 'f_' before each one to avoid confusion with our English parser), the only difference will be in one of the rules which deals with a noun phrase. This arises in the case where an adjective is used; here, we have seen that in French the adjective comes after the noun, whereas in English it comes before it. In the predicate which parses this form of French noun phrase, the checks are applied to different words to reflect this new order, as shown in the following definition:

```
f_noun_phrase ([Art, Nn, Adj| Out], Out) :-
    f_article (Art),
    f_noun (Nn),
    f_adjective (Adj).
```

This is the only essential difference between the parser for French sentences and our earlier English sentence parser. This gives the program shown below, which parses simple French sentences. It should be fairly straightforward to follow. This one is called Program 3.

```
f_sentence (In, Out) :-
     f_noun_phrase (In, Temp),
     f_verb_phrase (Temp, Out).

f_noun_phrase ([Art, Adj, Nn| Out], Out) :-
     f_article (Art),
     f_adjective (Adj),
     f_noun (Nn).

f_noun_phrase ([Art, Nn| Out], Out) :-
     f_article (Art),
     f_noun (Nn).

f_noun_phrase ([Name| Out], Out) :-
     f_name (Name).

f_verb_phrase ([V| Temp], Out) :-
     f_verb (V),
     f_prep_phrase (Temp, Out).

f_verb_phrase ([V| Out], Out) :-
     f_verb (V).

f_prep_phrase ([Prep| Temp], Out) :-
     f_preposition (Prep),
     f_noun_phrase (Temp, Out).

f_prep_phrase (In, Out) :-
     f_noun_phrase (In, Out).


f_article          (un).
f_article          (une).
f_article          (le).
f_article          (la).
f_article          (les).
f_noun             (chat).
f_noun             (chats).
f_noun             (tapis).
f_name             (pierre).
f_verb             (est).
f_verb             (sont).
f_adjective        (noir).
f_adjective        (noire).
f_preposition      (sur).
```

Program 3 *A parser for simple French sentences*

Using this program, we can now check simple French sentences for correct structure and word order. For instance, the query:

```
?-f_sentence ([le, noir, chat,
                   est, sur, le, tapis], _).
```

will fail within `f_noun_phrase`, when testing the condition:

```
f_noun (noir)
```

However, given a suitably extended vocabulary, our program would happily accept sentences such as:

pierre mange le chats

This would happen even though *le chats* is bad grammar in French. It should of course be *les chats*, because *le* is singular, whereas *chats* is plural. To get proper number agreement, a plural article is needed — hence *les*. This leads us on to the next section, which considers this problem of checking other grammatical points in French sentences.

6.6   Checking for good grammar in French

In checking for good grammar in English, the only point considered was that of number agreement. In French, there will be two aspects of good grammar which have to be allowed for:

(i) *Number agreement.* Just as in English, we have to check that the number of nouns, verbs and articles all agree. The rules for French, though, are more wide-ranging than for English, since French distinguishes between singular adjectives and plural adjectives. For instance, the word *noir* describes just one black thing, whereas if several black things were being described, then the word *noirs* would have to be used instead.

(ii) *Gender.* A much bigger difference in French, however, is that nouns, articles and adjectives can be either *masculine* or *feminine*; they are said to have *gender*. The gender of nouns, adjectives and articles must all agree. Thus, for instance, it would be wrong to say *la chat*, because in French *chat* is a masculine noun, but *la* is feminine. Similarly, to describe a black cat in French, it would be wrong to say *le chat noire*, since *noire* is the feminine form of the adjective for black. The masculine form is *noir*, so we should say *le chat noir*. The fact that things can now be either singular or plural, and either masculine or feminine, means that often there are four French words for the same English word. Take the case of the adjective black:

noir	describes one black masculine thing
noire	describes one black feminine thing
noirs	describes several black masculine things
noires	describes several black feminine things

When defining each French word in the vocabulary section, we must now include both number and gender information, where appropriate.

Extending the vocabulary with number and gender

Most types of French words will have both number and gender, but not all:

articles	will have both number and gender
nouns	will have both number and gender
names	will have both number and gender
adjectives	will have both number and gender
verbs	will just have number
prepositions	will have neither number nor gender

This will require the basic defining predicates to be extended; the predicate for French articles, for instance, will now become:

```
f_article (word, number, gender)
```

where gender will be denoted by either m for masculine or f for feminine. The earlier French vocabulary can now be defined with number and gender as follows:

```
f_article       (un,      s, m).
f_article       (une,     s, f).
f_article       (le,      s, m).
f_article       (la,      s, f).
f_article       (les,     p, m).
f_article       (les,     p, f).
f_noun          (chat,    s, m).
f_noun          (chats,   p, m).
f_noun          (tapis,   s, m).
f_noun          (tapis,   p, m).
f_name          (pierre,  s, m).
f_verb          (est,     s).
f_verb          (sont,    p).
f_adjective     (noir,    s, m).
f_adjective     (noire,   s, f).
f_adjective     (noirs,   p, m).
f_adjective     (noires,  p, f).
f_preposition   (sur).
...
```

Extending the parser with number and gender

Recall that when modifying the English parser to include checks for number agreement, we added an additional argument to the predicate for each structure which could be said to have an associated number. To add number and gender to the predicates in our existing French parser, we first have to identify those structures in simple French which have either number or gender:

> *noun phrases*   have both number and gender
> *verb phrases*   have just number
> *preposition phrases*   have neither number nor gender

Consider, for instance, the first case of a noun phrase in the French grammar:

> *f_noun_phrase = f_article f_noun f_adjective*

Here, both the number and the gender of all three words must agree; and the common number and gender will be returned as the number and gender of the overall noun phrase. This would be defined by the predicate:

```
f_noun_phrase ([Art, Nn, Adj| Out], Out,
                                        N, G):-
        f_article (Art, N, G),
        f_noun (Nn, N, G),
        f_adjective (Adj, N, G).
```

where N is the common number, and G is the common gender. Strictly speaking, for our simple grammar there is no need to return the overall gender of a noun phrase, since this gender is never used outside the noun phrase. However, we have included it here since a noun phrase does have a gender whether or not the gender is used. This predicate will therefore be able to trap grammatical errors, as in the query:

```
?-f_noun_phrase ([le, chat, noire], Out, N, G).
```

This will fail on the third condition, by which time N will have been set to s, and G will have been set to m. The third condition then turns out to be:

```
f_adjective (noire, s, m)
```

A glance at the definition of noire in the vocabulary shows that this will fail.

Similar extensions to the remaining predicates complete the checking process, and give the program shown below, Program 4. This program parses simple French sentences, and also does grammatical checking for number and gender agreement.

```
f_sentence (In, Out) :-
    f_noun_phrase (In, Temp, N, _),
    f_verb_phrase (Temp, Out, N).


f_noun_phrase ([Art, Adj, Nn| Out], Out,
                                    N, G) :-
    f_article (Art, N, G),
    f_adjective (Adj, N, G),
    f_noun (Nn, N, G).

f_noun_phrase ([Art, Nn| Out], Out, N, G) :-
    f_article (Art, N, G),
    f_noun (Nn, N, G).

f_noun_phrase ([Name| Out], Out, N, G) :-
    f_name (Name, N, G).


f_verb_phrase ([V| Temp], Out, N) :-
    f_verb (V, N),
    f_prep_phrase (Temp, Out).

f_verb_phrase ([V| Out], Out, N) :-
    f_verb (V, N).


f_prep_phrase ([Prep| Temp], Out) :-
    f_preposition (Prep),
    f_noun_phrase (Temp, Out, _, _).

f_prep_phrase (In, Out) :-
    f_noun_phrase (In, Out, _, _).


f_article            (un,      s, m).
f_article            (une,     s, f).
f_article            (le,      s, m).
f_article            (la,      s, f).
f_article            (les,     p, m).
f_article            (les,     p, f).
f_noun               (chat,    s, m).
f_noun               (chats,   p, m).
f_noun               (tapis,   s, m).
f_name               (pierre,  s, m).
f_verb               (est,     s).
f_verb               (sont,    p).
f_adjective          (noir,    s, m).
```

```
f_adjective          (noire,   s, f).
f_adjective          (noirs,   p, m).
f_adjective          (noires,  p, f).
f_preposition        (sur).
```

Program 4   *A parser and checker for simple French sentences*

6.7   Beginning the task of translation

If we are working in a multilingual environment, where each language has
to be translated into all the others, we can end up needing rather a lot of
translators:

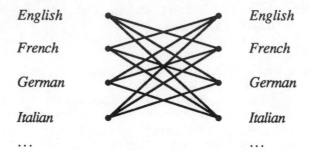

For say, nine languages in the EEC, this appears to need seventy-two
different translation specialists: each language has to be translated into eight
others, so for nine languages this gives nine times eight, which is seventy-
two. If a translator can translate in both directions, then this number is
halved, to thirty-six, since a French to English translator can double up as
an English to French translator.

A more sensible solution might be to do the translation in *two* stages.
If the translation is from some source language into another destination
language, these two stages would be:

- Translate the source language into some agreed intermediate language
  format.
- Translate this intermediate format into the destination language.

The scheme is then as shown opposite.

Let us call the intermediate language I. So when translating from some
source language, the document is first translated into the intermediate
language I. This requires nine 'X to I' translation specialists, where X can
be any one of the nine languages. Then this version in the intermediate
language is translated into each of the other languages. This requires
another nine specialists. Therefore, the number of specialists required
using this approach is only eighteen, or nine if the specialists can translate
in both directions. This compares rather favourably with seventy-two (or

thirty-six). Things also become much more simple if another language has to be added to the group. All that is required in this case is a further two specialists. This may even reduce to a single specialist who can translate in both directions between the new language and the intermediate language.

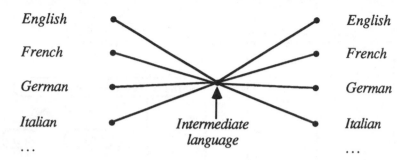

Choice of an intermediate language

What should this intermediate language be like? Should it be a totally separate and artificial language, such as Esperanto? For convenience rather than anything else, it would seem reasonable to take one of the actual languages as the 'intermediate' language. For instance, we could decide to choose English. This would mean that to translate a document from, say, French into German, the approach is to translate the document first from French into English, and then from English into German. In making this decision, there is the risk that something which can be expressed in French and in German cannot be expressed accurately in English. This would mean the translation would lose something in going through an English version on the way. But if we are not too concerned about losing some of the subtleties of meaning in the bureaucratic documents in question, then for our purposes in this chapter, this is a risk worth taking. It should be borne in mind, however, that in a more realistic system, this decision could lead to difficulties.

When doing the translation by computer, we will find things easier if we do not choose ordinary English *text* as the intermediate form. We have already seen that to get anywhere when translating a list of words, it is necessary to analyse the structure of the sentence. Analysing the structure, and remembering this structure, can be thought of as translating the free text version into a structured version. The structured version of a piece of text can be remembered and drawn as the *structure tree*, or *parse tree*, for the text. For instance, given the English sentence, in the text form:

 the black cat is on the mat

this would be 'translated' into a representation which we will call *Structured English*, represented by the tree:

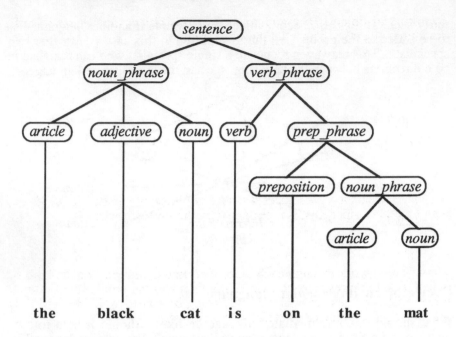

We will therefore adopt this Structured English as the agreed intermediate representation throughout the rest of this chapter. Translation of a sentence from English to French will be done in two stages:

- Building the structure tree from the English text version of the sentence; this will require parsing of the sentence, and some way of recording the structure which is recognised.
- Translating this structured representation into French text.

First we will look at the easier task of how to build an English structure tree from an English sentence, by extending our parser program so that it builds a description of the structure tree as the various parts of the sentence are recognised by the parser program. Then the more difficult task of translating between an English structure tree and a French text form of the sentence will be tackled. This is the section where the real translation is done.

6.8   Building a structure tree from English

We can already *recognise* the different components of an English sentence, using our parser program. Now all we have to do is to build a Prolog structure for every part which is recognised.

A component of a structure tree can be represented in Prolog as a structured object. Each different kind of structure will be represented by its own kind of object. The components of this object may themselves be structured objects. In general, the structure tree:

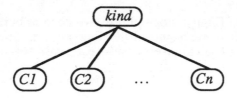

which represents a grammatical structure or phrase of a particular kind, and with several components, is represented by the Prolog object:

```
kind(C1, C2, ..., Cn)
```

We will now work through each kind of structure, and outline the kind of object used to represent each case. Only then will the problem of building these structure trees automatically in Prolog be considered. We will start with the simplest kind of structure — a basic word.

Representing basic words

Each word will be held as a simple structure, which specifies the type of word it is and what the word itself is. Each kind of word is represented in Prolog by its own kind of structured object, as shown below.

Word recognised	Prolog representation
cat	noun(cat)
is	verb(is)
the	article(the)
peter	name(peter)
on	preposition(on)

Representing higher level structures

The object representations which are built for individual words as shown above must be put together to build higher level object descriptions of phrases and structures within a sentence. Consider each kind of structure in turn.

Noun phrases

When we parse an English noun phrase, we need to build a tree structure which will hold the components of the noun phrase. Since there are three different cases of a noun phrase, consider each case separately.

1st case: *noun_phrase = article adjective noun*

A noun phrase of this type will be represented by structured object with three components:

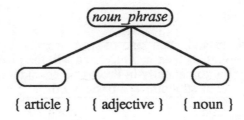

A Prolog object which represents this would be:

        noun_phrase(Article, Adjective, Noun)

For instance, the phrase:

   the black cat

would be represented by the tree:

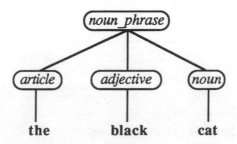

which in Prolog would be the object:

```
noun_phrase(article(the),
            adjective(black),
            noun(cat))
```

2nd case: *noun_phrase = article noun*

A representation of this type of noun phrase appears to have two components. However, to avoid confusion between a *noun_phrase* object with three components and one with two, we will regard this second case as though the adjective is missing, and fill up the vacant adjective position in the object with a dummy component. The result is a standard representation for noun phrases which always have three components. We can call this dummy component whatever we want, say `nil`. This gives a structure tree for this second type of noun phrase as follows:

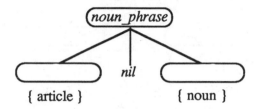

3rd case: *noun_phrase = name*

There is no need to build a higher level tree which has only one component. Just use the tree which was built for the name.

Verb phrases

1st case: *verb_phrase = verb prep_phrase*

The structure tree for this form of phrase is:

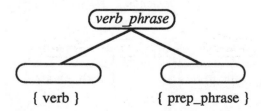

which is represented in Prolog by the object:

```
verb_phrase(Verb, Prep_phrase)
```

2nd case: *verb_phrase = verb*

Just return the tree built for the verb.

Preposition phrases

1st case: *prep_phrase = preposition noun_phrase*

The structure tree for this type of phrase is:

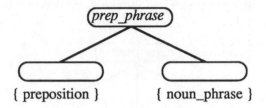

This is represented in Prolog by the object:

```
prep_phrase(Preposition, Noun_phrase)
```

2nd case: *prep_phrase = noun_phrase*

Again, it is sufficient to return the tree for *noun_phrase*.

Sentences

The tree for a complete sentence has two components:

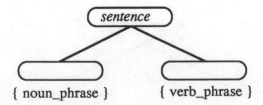

which can be held in Prolog as the object:

```
sentence(Noun_phrase, Verb_phrase)
```

Building the structure tree automatically

To get a Prolog program which builds these forms of structure tree from a list of English words, we go back to our English parser and checker program, Program 2. This program analyses, or recognises, the different structures within the sentence, so all we need to do is to make simple extensions to each clause to build the tree for the structure which the clause recognises. This is done clause by clause. Thus, every clause in the parser program will now have one extra argument, which will define the tree for the structure it parses. Also, to avoid confusion with the French parser clauses, we will put the prefix 'e_' at the front of each clause name in the English parser. So consider the predicates in Program 2 now to be called:

```
e_sentence
e_noun_phrase
e_verb_phrase
e_prep_phrase
e_article
e_noun
...
```

From the above example trees, a structure tree will have to be built even for basic words such as nouns and verbs.

Building the structure tree for words automatically

We could define the tree for each word within the vocabulary, but this would obscure the vocabulary section. Instead, introduce an intermediate level which builds a tree for each kind of basic word. This involves some simple changes in the way the vocabulary is defined:

(i) Change the vocabulary predicate names by adding a suffix '_e' on to each defining predicate of English words. This means that the vocabulary will now be defined using the following renamed set of basic predicates:

```
article_e      (Word, Number)
noun_e         (Word, Number)
name_e         (Word, Number)
verb_e         (Word, Number)
preposition_e  (Word)
```

(ii) Define new clauses for what had been the old basic predicates, now called e_article, and so on. These new predicates will not only check the individual word, but also return the structure tree for the word. For instance, the new definition for e_noun, which previously had just looked up the vocabulary, is now as follows:

```
e_noun (Word, Number, noun(Word)) :-
    noun_e (Word, Number).
```

For instance, the query:

```
?-e_noun (cat, s, Tree).
```

would succeed, and return the answer:

```
Tree = noun(cat)
```

which is exactly the structure tree we require. Likewise, each of the other basic word predicates can be redefined, as follows:

```
e_verb (Word, Number, verb(Word)) :-
    verb_e (Word, Number).

e_name (Word, Number, name(Word)) :-
    name_e (Word, Number).

e_article (Word, Number, article(Word)) :-
    article_e (Word, Number).

e_adjective (Word, adjective(Word)) :-
    adjective_e (Word).

e_preposition (Word, preposition(Word)) :-
    preposition_e (Word).
```

These clauses will build structure trees for each of the basic words. Now consider the higher level structures.

Building trees for phrases

The clauses which we currently have in Program 2 for recognising the various structures within a sentence now need to be extended to build the structure tree for each structure which is recognised. We have already defined the form of tree desired in each case, so it is now a simple matter to incorporate the building of the tree into each clause.

Noun phrases

Previously, the predicate e_noun_phrase had three arguments: the input list of words, the output list, and the number. Now a fourth is added — the structure tree for the noun phrase. Again, consider each of the three types of noun phrase separately.

1st case: *noun_phrase = article adjective noun*

The predicate has now also to build a *noun_phrase* object with three
components: the trees for the article (called `Art_tree`), the adjective
(`Adj_tree`) and noun (`Nn_tree`).

```
e_noun_phrase ([Art, Adj, Nn| Out], Out, N,
                        noun_phrase(Art_tree,
                                    Adj_tree,
                                    Nn_tree)) :-
        e_article   (Art, N, Art_tree),
        e_adjective (Adj, Adj_tree),
        e_noun      (Nn,  N, Nn_tree).
```

2nd case: *noun_phrase = article noun*

The tree to be built is a *noun_phrase* object with three components: the
article and noun trees, and a dummy tree for the 'missing' adjective (`nil`):

```
e_noun_phrase ([Art, Nn| Out], Out, N,
                noun_phrase (Art_tree,
                             nil,
                             Nn_tree)) :-
        e_article (Art, N, Art_tree),
        e_noun    (Nn,  N, Nn_tree).
```

3rd case: *noun_phrase = name*

The tree which is returned is merely the tree constructed for the name:
```
e_noun_phrase ([Name| Out], Out, N, Tree) :-
        e_name (Name, N, Tree).
```

Verb phrases

1st case: *verb_phrase = verb prep_phrase*

The previous predicate must now have an extra, fourth argument, which is
the tree for a verb phrase of this form:

```
e_verb_phrase ([V| Temp], Out, N,
                verb_phrase(V_tree, P_tree)) :-
        e_verb (V, N, V_tree),
        e_prep_phrase (Temp, Out, P_tree).
```

2nd case: *verb_phrase = verb*

The tree returned in this case is just the tree built for the verb, called
`V_tree`:

```
e_verb_phrase ([V| Out], Out, N, V_tree) :-
    e_verb (V, N, V_tree).
```

Preposition phrases

1st case: *prep_phrase = preposition noun_phrase*

The previous predicate, which had two arguments, now has a third, which is the object built to represent the structure tree for the preposition phrase:

```
e_prep_phrase ([Prep| Temp], Out,
               prep_phrase(P_tree, Np_tree)) :-
    e_preposition (Prep, P_tree),
    e_noun_phrase (Temp, Out, _, Np_tree).
```

2nd case: *prep_phrase = noun_phrase*

Since this is another case which has no new structure, the tree for the preposition is just the tree for the noun phrase:

```
e_prep_phrase (In, Out, Tree) :-
    e_noun_phrase (In, Out, _, Tree).
```

Sentences

The last clause to be extended to build the tree representation is that for processing a sentence. This builds an object with two components: the trees for the noun phrase (N_tree) and verb phrase (V_tree):

```
e_sentence (In, Out,
            sentence(N_tree, V_tree)) :-
    e_noun_phrase (In, Temp, N, N_tree),
    e_verb_phrase (Temp, Out, N, V_tree).
```

The complete tree-building program

Putting all these clauses together, and adding the vocabulary, gives a complete program which parses an English sentence, checks it, and builds the structure tree for it. This is Program 5.

```
e_sentence (In, Out,
            sentence(N_tree, V_tree)) :-
    e_noun_phrase (In, Temp, N, N_tree),
    e_verb_phrase (Temp, Out, N, V_tree).
```

```
e_noun_phrase ([Art, Adj, Nn| Out], Out, N,
                       noun_phrase(Art_tree,
                                   Adj_tree,
                                   Nn_tree)) :-
    e_article   (Art, N, Art_tree),
    e_adjective (Adj, Adj_tree),
    e_noun      (Nn, N, Nn_tree).

e_noun_phrase ([Art, Nn| Out], Out, N,
                       noun_phrase(Art_tree,
                                   nil,
                                   Nn_tree)) :-
    e_article (Art, N, Art_tree),
    e_noun    (Nn, N, Nn_tree).

e_noun_phrase ([Name| Out], Out, N, Tree) :-
    e_name (Name, N, Tree).

e_verb_phrase ([V| Temp], Out, N,
               verb_phrase(V_tree, P_tree)) :-
    e_verb (V, N, V_tree),
    e_prep_phrase (Temp, Out, P_tree).

e_verb_phrase ([V| Out], Out, N, V_tree) :-
    e_verb (V, N, V_tree).

e_prep_phrase ([Prep| Temp], Out,
            prep_phrase(P_tree, Np_tree)) :-
    e_preposition (Prep, P_tree),
    e_noun_phrase (Temp, Out, _, Np_tree).

e_prep_phrase (In, Out, Tree) :-
    e_noun_phrase (In, Out, _, Tree).


e_noun (Word, Number, noun(Word)) :-
    noun_e (Word, Number).

e_verb (Word, Number, verb(Word)) :-
    verb_e (Word, Number).

e_name (Word, Number, name(Word)) :-
    name_e (Word, Number).

e_article (Word, Number, article(Word)) :-
    article_e (Word, Number).

e_adjective (Word, adjective(Word)) :-
    adjective_e (Word).
```

```
e_preposition (Word, preposition(Word)) :-
    preposition_e (Word).
```

```
article_e          (the,    s).
article_e          (the,    p).
article_e          (a,      s).
noun_e             (cat,    s).
noun_e             (cats,   p).
noun_e             (mat,    s).
noun_e             (mats,   p).
name_e             (fred,   s).
name_e             (peter,  s).
adjective_e        (black).
adjective_e        (furry).
adjective_e        (wet).
verb_e             (is,     s).
verb_e             (are,    p).
verb_e             (barked, s).
verb_e             (barked, p).
preposition_e      (on).
```

Program 5   *A tree-building program for simple English sentences*

As an example of this program's operation, consider the following query:

```
?-e_sentence ([the, black, cat,
               is, on, the, mat], [], Tree).
```

This query will succeed, and will produce the representation of the structure tree as a Prolog object Tree as shown below. The layout of the object has been indented to make its structure more clear:

```
Tree = sentence(
           noun_phrase(
               article(the),
               adjective(black),
               noun(cat)),
           verb_phrase(
               verb(is),
               prep_phrase(
                   preposition(on),
                   noun_phrase(
                       article(the),
                       nil,
                       noun(mat))))))
```

The correspondence between this object and the parse tree of the input sentence can be seen from the following diagram:

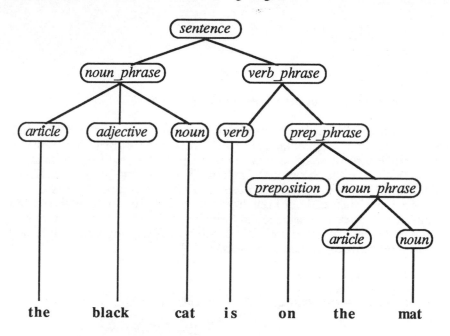

Using the program backwards

Program 5 has an interesting property. We normally expect to supply the sentence as a list of words, and get back the structure tree. But, just as our dictionary program was two-way (English–French, or French–English), so too this program is two-way. We can supply the structure tree, and get back the list of words corresponding to the supplied tree! For example, the query:

```
?-e_sentence (L, sentence(name(fred),
                          verb(barked))).
```

would succeed, and produce as the answer the list of words which would have been required to produce the supplied tree:

```
L = [fred, barked]
```

Or, consider the query:

```
?-e_noun_phrase (L, N,
                 noun_phrase(article(a),
                             nil,
                             noun(man))).
```

This would respond with the list of words which would have produced the supplied tree:

```
L = [a, man]
N = s
```

6.9   Building a structure tree from French

The structure tree built by the extended English parser translates English text into the intermediate 'language' of Structured English. To translate from French into some other language, the first stage will be to translate from French text into Structured English: in other words, to input a list of French words, and produce a representation in Structured English. We therefore want to extend our French parser so that it not only analyses and checks the structure of a sentence in French, but also builds a structure tree for the sentence. Together with our English tree-building parser, this will give us the following system of parsers:

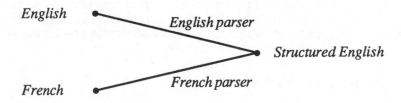

Since the structured tree representation is a common intermediate form, then the structured English form of the English sentence:

> *the black cat is on the mat*

has to be the same as the structured English form of the equivalent sentence in French:

> *le chat noir est sur le tapis*

Thus, our extended French parser, which produces an English structure tree from a list of French words, must contain *English* words, rather than French words. In other words, given a final structure tree, it should be impossible to detect whether it was produced from a list of French words or from a list of English words (or from any other language for that matter). Thus, for instance, the French noun phrase:

> *le chat noir*

will be represented by the structure tree:

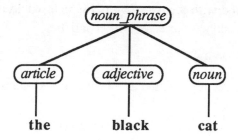

Thus, it is in this process of building a Structured English representation from a French sentence where the real translation work is done.

Building structures for basic French words

The vocabulary-defining primitives (f_noun, f_verb, and so on) have now to be modified to return a tree for each basic word. Again, the clause which builds the tree for the word has to be separated out from the actual definition of the word itself in the vocabulary, since the vocabulary proper does not define the structure tree for each word. So, between the vocabulary and the parser we interpose a set of simple predicates which build the structure tree for each French word. This is exactly what we did before for English. Again, we rename the vocabulary predicates, from f_noun, f_verb, and so on, to be noun_f, verb_f, etc. These old names, such as f_noun, are used for the intermediate tree-building predicates. The vocabulary itself now becomes:

```
article_f       (un,      s, m).
article_f       (une,     s, f).
article_f       (le,      s, m).
article_f       (la,      s, f).
article_f       (les,     p, m).
article_f       (les,     p, f).
noun_f          (chat,    s, m).
noun_f          (chats,   p, m).
noun_f          (tapis,   s, m).
name_f          (pierre,  s, m).
verb_f          (est,     s).
verb_f          (sont,    p).
adjective_f     (noir,    s, m).
adjective_f     (noire,   s, f).
adjective_f     (noirs,   p, m).
adjective_f     (noires,  p, f).
preposition_f   (sur).
. . .
```

Now consider what English structure trees have to be built for each type of basic word. For instance, for *chat*, which satisfies:

```
noun_f (chat, s, m)
```

the corresponding tree represented as a Prolog object should be:

```
noun(cat)
```

To construct this object, we will obviously need to know the English word which corresponds to each French word. Previously, this was specified using the predicate means:

```
means (chat, cat).
means (noir, black).
means (noire, black).
means (le, the).
...
```

However, we now need to be able to distinguish between the different cases where one French word has two possible English translations (or vice versa). For instance, *tapis* could be translated by either of the English words *mat* or *mats*. To choose the right English word to store in the tree, it is best to include the English translation of a French word in the vocabulary. Including this as an extra component gives the revised vocabulary:

```
article_f        (un,       s, m, a).
article_f        (une,      s, f, a).
article_f        (le,       s, m, the).
article_f        (la,       s, f, the).
article_f        (les,      p, m, the).
article_f        (les,      p, f, the).
noun_f           (chat,     s, m, cat).
noun_f           (chats,    p, m, cats).
noun_f           (tapis,    s, m, mat).
noun_f           (tapis,    p, m, mats).
name_f           (pierre,   s, m, peter).
verb_f           (est,      s,    is).
verb_f           (sont,     p,    are).
adjective_f      (noir,     s, m, black).
adjective_f      (noire,    s, f, black).
adjective_f      (noirs,    p, m, black).
adjective_f      (noires,   p, f, black).
preposition_f    (sur,         on).
...
```

In general, the (English) structure tree for any French noun is now defined by a predicate:

```
f_noun (French word,  number,  gender,  structure tree)
```

which can be defined in full by:

```
f_noun (F_word, N, G, noun(E_word)) :-
     noun_f (F_word, N, G, E_word).
```

For instance:

```
?-f_noun (tapis, N, G, Tree).
```

would produce the response:

```
N = s
G = m
Tree = noun(mat)
```

The predicates for the other types of French word can be defined similarly:

```
f_article (F_word, N, G, article(E_word)) :-
     article_f (F_word, N, G, E_word).

f_name (F_word, N, G, name(E_word)) :-
     name_f (F_word, N, G, E_word).

f_verb (F_word, N, verb(E_word)) :-
     verb_f (F_word, N, E_word).

f_adjective (F_word, N, G, adjective(E_word)) :-
     adjective_f (F_word, N, G, E_word).

f_preposition (F_word, preposition(E_word)) :-
     preposition_f (F_word, E_word).
```

Building trees for French phrases

Now consider the higher level trees which are built using the basic trees for individual French words. For each clause in the French parser, we add an extra parameter, which is the Structured English tree to be built. Consider each clause in turn.

Noun phrases

1st case: *f_noun_phrase = f_article f_noun f_adjective*

Remember that the tree built from a French noun phrase must be exactly the same as the tree built from the equivalent English noun phrase. Therefore, although the order in the French text is different from English, the three components must be stored in the tree in the same order as they are in English. This order was: article, adjective, noun. Extending the earlier clause for parsing and checking French noun phrases of this form gives the following clause:

```
f_noun_phrase ([Art, Nn, Adj| Out], Out, N, G,
                          noun_phrase(Art_tree,
                                      Adj_tree,
                                      Nn_tree)) :-
        f_article (Art, N, G, Art_tree),
        f_noun     (Nn, N, G, Nn_tree),
        f_adjective (Adj, N, G, Adj_tree).
```

It should be obvious from this that the tree object returned for the input list:

```
[le, chat, noir]
```

is:

```
noun_phrase(article(the),
            adjective(black),
            noun(cat))
```

2nd case: *f_noun_phrase = f_article f_noun*

To make sure that both types of *noun_phrase* object have three components, the 'missing' adjective should have its position filled with the dummy object nil:

```
f_noun_phrase ([Art, Nn| Out], Out, N, G,
                          noun_phrase(Art_tree,
                                      nil,
                                      Nn_tree)) :-
        f_article (Art, N, G, Art_tree),
        f_noun     (Nn, N, G, Nn_tree).
```

3rd case: *f_noun_phrase = f_name*

The tree for this form of noun phrase is just the tree for the name:

```
f_noun_phrase ([Name| Out], Out, N, G, Tree) :-
        f_name (Name, N, G, Tree).
```

The complete tree-building program

This tree construction process can now be applied systematically to each remaining clause in the previous French parser and checker, Program 4. This results in the following Prolog program, called Program 6.

```
f_sentence (In, Out,
            sentence(N_tree, V_tree)) :-
     f_noun_phrase (In, Temp, N, _, N_tree),
     f_verb_phrase (Temp, Out, N, V_tree).

f_noun_phrase ([Art, Nn, Adj| Out], Out, N, G,
                    noun_phrase(Art_tree,
                                Adj_tree,
                                Nn_tree)) :-
     f_article (Art, N, G, Art_tree),
     f_noun    (Nn, N, G, Nn_tree),
     f_adjective (Adj, N, G, Adj_tree).

f_noun_phrase ([Art, Nn| Out], Out, N, G,
                    noun_phrase(Art_tree,
                                nil,
                                Nn_tree)) :-
     f_article (Art, N, G, Art_tree),
     f_noun    (Nn, N, G, Nn_tree).

f_noun_phrase ([Name| Out], Out, N, G, Tree) :-
     f_name (Name, N, G, Tree).

f_verb_phrase ([V| Temp], Out, N,
               verb_phrase(V_tree, P_tree)):-
     f_verb (V, N, V_tree),
     f_prep_phrase (Temp, Out, P_tree).

f_verb_phrase ([V| Out], Out, N, V_tree) :-
     f_verb (V, N, V_tree).

f_prep_phrase ([Prep| Temp], Out,
               prep_phrase(P_tree, N_tree)):-
     f_preposition (Prep, P_tree),
     f_noun_phrase (Temp, Out, _, _, N_tree).

f_prep_phrase (In, Out, P_tree) :-
     f_noun_phrase (In, Out, _, _, P_tree).


f_noun (F_word, N, G, noun(E_word)) :-
     noun_f (F_word, N, G, E_word).

f_article (F_word, N, G, article(E_word)) :-
     article_f (F_word, N, G, E_word).

f_name (F_word, N, G, name(E_word)) :-
     name_f (F_word, N, G, E_word).
```

```
f_verb (F_word, N, verb(E_word)) :-
     verb_f (F_word, N, E_word).

f_adjective (F_word, N, G, adjective(E_word)):-
     adjective_f (F_word, N, G, E_word).

f_preposition (F_word, preposition(E_word)):-
     preposition_f (F_word, E_word).


article_f          (un,      s, m, a).
article_f          (une,     s, f, a).
article_f          (le,      s, m, the).
article_f          (la,      s, f, the).
article_f          (les,     p, m, the).
article_f          (les,     p, f, the).
noun_f             (chat,    s, m, cat).
noun_f             (chats,   p, m, cats).
noun_f             (tapis,   s, m, mat).
noun_f             (tapis,   p, m, mats).
name_f             (pierre,  s, m, peter).
verb_f             (est,     s,    is).
verb_f             (sont,    p,    are).
adjective_f        (noir,    s, m, black).
adjective_f        (noire,   s, f, black).
adjective_f        (noirs,   p, m, black).
adjective_f        (noires,  p, f, black).
preposition_f      (sur,        on).
```

Program 6 *A tree builder for simple French sentences*

Again, this program has the interesting two-way property that, if it is given the English structure tree instead of the list of French words, it will generate the list of French words which would have given the supplied structure tree. For instance, the query:

```
?-f_sentence (L, [],
                 sentence(
                    name(peter),
                    verb_phrase(
                       verb(is),
                       noun_phrase(article(a),
                                   nil,
                                   noun(cat))))).
```

would reply with the answer:

```
L = [pierre, est, un, chat]
```

6.10   The final step

We now have two parsing programs, each of which builds the same type of structure tree from a list of words:

(i) Program 5 translates between English text and Structured English. Note that the translation can be either way, because of the reversible nature of the Prolog program.
(ii) Program 6 translates between French text and Structured English. Note that this program can also operate either way.

These two programs are the key to doing translation in either direction between French and English.

French to English

To obtain a translator between French text and English text is now quite straightforward: we put both these programs together. A French to English translation will be done in the following two stages:

• Translate the French text into Structured English, using Program 6.
• Use Program 5 in reverse mode, to translate the Structured English version into English text.

This operation can be defined by a new predicate:

```
french_to_english (French, English) :-
       f_sentence (French, [], Tree),
       e_sentence (English, [], Tree).
```

This predicate takes an input list of French words, parses them as a sentence, and builds the Structured English version, called Tree; then the use of e_sentence takes this tree and finds the list of English words which corresponds to this tree. For instance, the query:

```
?-french_to_english
                ([pierre, est, un, chat], E).
```

first builds the Prolog object Tree:

```
sentence(name(peter),
         verb_phrase(verb(is),
                          noun_phrase(article(a),
                                      nil,
                                      noun(cat))))
```

This tree is then supplied to the predicate e_sentence, which returns the corresponding list of English words:

```
E = [peter, is, a, cat]
```

English to French

An English to French translation will likewise be done in the following two stages:

- Translate the English text into the corresponding Structured English format, using Program 5.
- Use Program 6 in reverse mode, to translate the Structured English version into French text.

This operation can be defined by the following predicate:

```
english_to_french (English, French) :-
        e_sentence (English, [], Tree),
        f_sentence (French, [], Tree).
```

This predicate takes an input list of English words, parses them as a sentence, and builds the Structured English version, called `Tree`; then, the use of `f_sentence` takes this tree and finds the list of French words which corresponds to this tree. For instance, the query:

```
?-english_to_french
                ([the, cat, is, on, the, mat], F).
```

first produces the Structured English version represented by the object `Tree`:

```
sentence(noun_phrase(article(the),
                     nil,
                     noun(cat)),
        verb_phrase(verb(is),
                    prep_phrase(
                        preposition(on),
                        noun_phrase(
                            article(the),
                            nil,
                            noun(mat))))))
```

When passed to the predicate `f_sentence`, the reversible property of this predicate will generate the equivalent list of French words:

```
F = [le, chat, est, sur, le, tapis]
```

Gathering together our new translation predicates gives the complete picture. The following program requires Program 5 and Program 6 to be included.

{ *... All predicates from Programs 5 and 6 included here ...* }

```
french_to_english (French, English) :-
    f_sentence (French, [], Tree),
    e_sentence (English, [], Tree).

english_to_french (English, French) :-
    e_sentence (English, [], Tree),
    f_sentence (French, [], Tree).
```

Program 7   *The complete English/French translation program*

A final word of warning

The approach to translation which we have adopted in this chapter still has many shortcomings. One immediate limitation is the simplicity of the English and French grammars and vocabularies. The vocabularies are not difficult to extend: this merely requires a new definition for each new word. Extending the grammar, however, is not so trivial. If we want to introduce a new sort of phrase, then a new predicate for this phrase must be defined; also, a new kind of structure in the Structured English tree must be invented to represent this new type of phrase; and finally, the translation from this Structured English version into the destination language(s) must be included.

Perhaps a more fundamental limitation of our program is its inability to understand the language it is processing. Often, to translate a particular word, it is necessary to know the context in which it is being used. This would make our simple dictionary approach to translating words using the predicate means fairly useless. An improved version of means would need to take the context into consideration. However, the structure tree which is already available does make quite a good basis for representing this context.

So for translating human language, or *natural language*, our program still has a long way to go; indeed, if the ultimate goal was to be able to translate full natural language, perhaps a radically different approach would be called for. However, the approach used in this chapter is definitely very useful for processing *artificial* languages: in particular, languages which are used to communicate with computers. One very common application in this area is the writing of *compilers*. A compiler is a program which translates a programming language into a lower level language which a machine can understand directly. Prolog is becoming increasingly popular in this area, and makes the processing of computer languages much more straightforward and convenient.

7

An application in law

It is difficult to live life in a society without encountering all sorts of rules and regulations. Whether or not we actually keep them, we still come across them. Rules and laws play a vital part in an ordered society, whether it be the Highway Code, social security regulations, tax laws, or whatever.

Laws as we know them tend to be written in their own rather specialised style and jargon. The reason for using this legal type of language, lawyers tell us, is to make the rules clear, precise, complete and unambiguous. This sometimes results in a rather technical form of language or legal jargon, which is clear, precise, complete and unambiguous only to legal experts. Consider the following fragment from the wording of the television licence application form from the Home Office:

> Except with the written consent of the Secretary of State, the apparatus for wireless telegraphy comprised in this licence (hereinafter called 'the apparatus') shall not be electrically coupled with apparatus for wireless telegraphy elsewhere than in the said premises (except a broadcast relay station licensed by the Secretary of State) or with such apparatus in any part of the said premises which is not in the occupation of the Licensee, or (where the said premises are a hotel, inn, boarding house, guest house, holiday camp or similar premises) with such apparatus in any room or accommodation which is let to a boarder or guest (not being the Licensee) or is usually available for being let to boarders or guests.

The rather convoluted style of legislation like this is no doubt necessary, given that every contingency must be allowed for, and every possible loophole must be closed. However, the end result of using a technical legal language to express laws is that, for the layman to understand the law, and to know whether or not he or she has broken it, a legal expert often needs to be called in to interpret the law. It is unfortunate (for the layman) that such services usually have to be paid for.

Recently, there has been interest in trying to take laws written in the usual legal language, and re-express them in a language which is still precise and unambiguous, but which can be interpreted without the aid of a legal expert. The language which some researchers have been looking at is Prolog. This may seem a little surprising, but there are quite good reasons for choosing Prolog, as we shall see. One group at Imperial College, London, has taken various sections of British Law, and re-expressed them in Prolog. We will look later at one of their projects: the British Nationality Act. But first, to introduce the idea, consider the following rather simpler example.

7.1   Ballymucknacreevy Jetsetters' Club

In an effort to preserve declining standards of excellence, the high fliers of Ballymucknacreevy have come together, and established an exclusive club. Among the many rules of the club is a section on the acceptability of potential new members. This section goes as follows:

RULES FOR ACCEPTANCE OF NEW MEMBERS

A person applying for membership of Ballymucknacreevy Jetsetters' Club (hereinafter referred to as the applicant) will be deemed acceptable for membership provided the applicant has been proposed by two other persons (hereinafter referred to as the proposers), each of whom is qualified to propose the aforementioned applicant, and provided the applicant is eligible for membership under the terms below.

The applicant must be less than 40 years of age.

A proposer is not qualified to propose a potential applicant if he or she earns less than $30,000, or if he or she has been a member of the Club for less than two years.

>*A proposer may not be a parent of the applicant.*
>
>*An applicant is eligible for membership if his or her annual salary is not less than $40,000. Alternatively, an applicant earning not less than $20,000 will be eligible provided a parent of the applicant would be eligible for membership under the above rules.*

Given these rules which define the conditions under which a person is acceptable for membership, we will now develop a set of Prolog rules which define the same thing. At the highest level, we require a predicate:

```
acceptable (Applicant) :- ...
```

which defines the conditions under which an applicant is acceptable for membership. From the above regulations, the applicant is acceptable provided:

- The applicant has two qualified proposers.
- The applicant is eligible for membership.
- The applicant is less than 40 years of age.

It is a simple matter at this stage to assume a predicate for each of these three conditions, leaving the details of the predicate definitions for later. This enables the definition of acceptable to be completed:

```
acceptable (Applicant) :-
     has_two_qualified_proposers (Applicant),
     eligible_for_membership (Applicant),
     age (Applicant, Age),
     Age < 40.
```

The third of these conditions (about the applicant's age) is assumed to be defined by a fact which specifies a personal detail of the person involved. Each of the other two new predicates now needs to be refined. Consider first the predicate, has_two_qualified_proposers.

Qualified proposers

From the rules of the club, the conditions under which an applicant has two qualified proposers can be expressed in Prolog as follows:

```
has_two_qualified_proposers (Applicant) :-
     has_proposed (Proposer1, Applicant),
```

```
has_proposed (Proposer2, Applicant),
not (Proposer1 = Proposer2),
qualified_to_propose (Proposer1,
                      Applicant),
qualified_to_propose (Proposer2,
                      Applicant).
```

The third of these conditions is necessary to ensure that the two proposers are in fact distinct people. Also, the predicate:

```
has_proposed (Proposer, Applicant)
```

is used to define the fact that `Proposer` has formally proposed `Applicant` for membership, irrespective of whether or not `Proposer` is in fact qualified to do this. Normally we would expect this just to be a blunt fact; if one day Fred Bloggs proposed Marilyn Monro for membership, then this fact could be specified by:

```
has_proposed (fred_bloggs, marilyn_monro).
```

Now consider the predicate:

```
qualified_to_propose (Proposer, Applicant)
```

This should succeed only if the proposer is actually qualified to propose the applicant. So under what conditions is someone qualified to propose an applicant? The regulations state when a person is *not* qualified; so inverting this gives the following conditions for the proposer being qualified to propose the applicant, all of which must be satisfied:

- The proposer must earn at least $30 000.
- The proposer must have been a member for at least two years.
- The proposer must not be a parent of Applicant.

To express this in Prolog requires certain facts giving personal information about the proposer, including:

- How much the proposer earns.
- When the proposer joined.
- Who the applicant's parents are.

This will require a Prolog definition of the personal details of each proposer and applicant. We assume this will be done by defining a set of facts, using the following predicates:

```
earns (Person, Salary)
joined_on_date (Person, Date)
parent_of (Person1, Person2)
```

Assuming this information to be defined as part of the program by a suitable set of facts, the predicate `qualified_to_propose` could be expressed in Prolog as:

```
qualified_to_propose (Proposer, Applicant) :-
    earns (Proposer, Salary),
    Salary >= 30000,
    joined_on_date (Proposer, D),
    at_least_two_years_ago (D),
    not (parent_of (Proposer, Applicant)).
```

Note that we have assumed a predicate:

```
at_least_two_years_ago (Date)
```

The definition of this predicate would have to consult today's date, and check that the supplied date was at least two years before today's date. This might be defined as follows:

```
at_least_two_years_ago (date(D, M, Y)) :-
    todays_date (Today),
    Y_plus_2 is Y + 2,
    not (after (date(D, M, Y_plus_2), Today)).
```

The definition of the predicate:

```
after (Date1, Date2)
```

which succeeds if `Date1` comes after `Date2`, is left as an exercise for the enthusiastic reader!

Eligibility for membership

The one predicate which now remains to be defined is:

```
eligible_for_membership (Applicant)
```

From the written regulations, there are two alternative conditions under which an applicant is eligible for membership — either:

• The applicant earns not less than $40 000.

or

• The applicant earns not less than $20 000
  and a parent of the applicant would be eligible.

In Prolog, we merely have a separate definition of the predicate `eligible_for_membership` for each of these alternatives. In the second case, to express the condition:

'... *a parent of the applicant would be eligible*'

requires a recursive use of the predicate eligible_for_membership. This will result in the salary of the applicant's parent being examined, and perhaps even the grandparent, and so on. The definition of the predicate eligible_for_membership is therefore as follows:

```
eligible_for_membership (Applicant) :-
     earns (Applicant, Salary),
     Salary >= 40000.

eligible_for_membership (Applicant) :-
     earns (Applicant, Salary),
     Salary >= 20000,
     parent_of (Parent, Applicant),
     eligible_for_membership (Parent).
```

This completes the Prolog definition of who is acceptable for membership.

The complete specification

If all the Prolog rules developed so far are gathered together, we obtain the program shown below. These Prolog statements have the same meaning as the English statements in the official *Rules for Acceptance of New Members*.

```
acceptable (Applicant) :-
     has_two_qualified_proposers (Applicant),
     eligible_for_membership (Applicant),
         age (Applicant, Age),
         Age < 40.

has_two_qualified_proposers (Applicant) :-
     has_proposed (Proposer1, Applicant),
     has_proposed (Proposer2, Applicant),
     not (Proposer1 = Proposer2),
     qualified_to_propose (Proposer1,
                              Applicant),
     qualified_to_propose (Proposer2,
                              Applicant).

qualified_to_propose (Proposer, Applicant) :-
     earns (Proposer, Salary),
     Salary >= 30000,
     Joined_on_date (Proposer, D),
     at_least_two_years_ago (D),
     not (parent_of (Proposer, Applicant)).
```

```
eligible_for_membership (Applicant) :-
     earns (Applicant, Salary),
     Salary >= 40000.

eligible_for_membership (Applicant) :-
     earns (Applicant, Salary),
     Salary >= 20000,
     parent_of (Parent, Applicant),
     eligible_for_membership (Parent).
```

7.2   Analysis of the Prolog definition

The Prolog formulation of the rules for new membership points to several advantages which Prolog could have as a way of expressing laws:

(i) *Clarification of ambiguities.* Due to lax phrasing, there is a slight ambiguity in the original formulation of who is qualified to propose an applicant. It is stated that:

> *'A proposer is not qualified to propose a potential applicant if he or she earns less than $30 000'*

Now, to whom does the *'he or she'* refer — the proposer, or the applicant? From the context we would guess it to be the proposer, but strictly speaking it is ambiguous. However, in the Prolog formulation this could not arise, since it must be made explicit by the use of variable names. Our Prolog definition states the condition as:

```
qualified_to_propose (Proposer, Applicant) :-
     earns (Proposer, Salary),
     Salary >= 30000,
     . . .
```

which clearly states that it is the proposer who is the *'he or she'*. If the rule had meant the applicant, the Prolog definition would have been:

```
qualified_to_propose (Proposer, Applicant) :-
     earns (Applicant, Salary),
     Salary >= 30000,
     . . .
```

Thus the Prolog definition is unambiguous. There is of course the danger that in constructing the Prolog version we *misinterpret* the original intention. However, if care is taken, it is more likely in practice that the ambiguity will be brought to our attention. Advice would then be sought from the legislators, and the Prolog rule formulated accordingly.

(ii) *Understandability*. In some ways, and with a bit of practice, a novice could well find it easier to read and understand a Prolog description of a law, rather than one in technical legal jargon. This may not be very apparent in the above example; but in much more complex legislation, as in the previous quotation, this might be more noticeable.

(iii) *Interpreting the definition*. If the Prolog facts mentioned previously about specific people were added to the definition, by giving suitable definitions of the following predicates:

```
has_proposed
age
earns
joined_on_date
parent_of
```

then we would have a complete Prolog program. Simply by asking the query, say:

```
?-acceptable (marilyn_monro).
```

the program would answer this by following the usual logical reasoning process. This would effectively interpret the law for us, and tell us whether Marilyn Monro was legally acceptable or not. A major advantage of this is that we now do not have to understand the law ourselves: the program is behaving like a legal expert, providing (cheap) advice to the user on points of law. On the face of it, things are looking ominous for our lawyer friends, since it seems to open up the possibility of having a computerised advice service which could perhaps take the place of legal advisers.

A word of caution is in order, however, before getting too excited about the possibilities of this type of approach. Our example is very small, very straightforward, and not truly representative of 'real' law. The idea needs to be tested on some pieces of real legislation, and judged by real users. For this reason, the next section outlines how a group of researchers at Imperial College adopted the Prolog approach to defining some actual law — in this case, the British Nationality Act. Our coverage will be far from complete, but it should illustrate something of the approach, and something of the problems, too.

7.3   The British Nationality Act

The British Nationality Act (1981) defines who is a British citizen (and, by default, who is not). Think of the UK as being a club, albeit a rather larger and less exclusive club than Ballymucknacreevy Jetsetters' Club. Then the rules defining British citizenship have certain parallels with the earlier rules for club membership in their intent.

The British Nationality Act consists of five Parts, defining different categories of citizenship, plus several odds and ends called Schedules. The first part, Part 1, defines standard British citizenship. Under Part 1 of the Act, it is possible to acquire British citizenship by six different routes:

- *By birth*:
    Some people are born citizens.
- *By adoption*:
    Some people become citizens by being adopted at some point in their life.
- *By descent*
- *At commencement*:
    Most people who had been citizens under the previous Act have now become citizens all over again when the new Act came into force.
- *By registration*
- *By naturalisation*

We will be considering only the first of these categories in any detail. What we wish to end up with is a predicate which defines the conditions under which a person is a British citizen:

```
citizen (X) :-  ...
```

Citizenship by birth

Since there are many different routes to citizenship, there will be many different rules defining various cases of the predicate `citizen`. As an example, consider the first clause of the Act:

> 1.-(1) A person born in the United Kingdom after commencement shall be a British citizen if at the time of birth his father or mother is:
> (a) a British citizen; or
> (b) settled in the United Kingdom.

where 'after commencement' means after or on the date on which the Act comes into force.

Restating this in a way which lists the conditions under which a person X is a British citizen (by section 1.-(1)) gives the following:

> *X is a British citizen if*
>> *X was born in the UK, and*
>> *X was born on date D, and*
>> *D is after or on commencement date, and*
>> *a parent of X is a British citizen or is settled in the UK*

Now let us try to express this in Prolog. This requires various predicates, some of which will define factual information about the people involved, such as where and when a person was born, and who their parents are. Doing this, and assuming for the minute whatever predicates we might need, gives the following:

```
citizen (X)  :-
      born_in (X, uk),
      born_on_date (X, Date),
      after_commencement (Date),
      parent_of (Parent, X),
      citizen_or_settled_in_UK (Parent).
```

where the predicate `after_commencement` succeeds if the supplied date is after or on the commencement date; it could be defined as follows:

```
after_commencement (Date)  :-
      commencement_date (Comm_date),
      after_or_on (Date, Comm_date).
```

The predicate `after_or_on` compares two dates, and will be rather similar to the predicate `after` which we met earlier.

The last condition of `citizen` involves an *or*, and would require two rules to define the two different cases. The first case, which tests if the parent is a British citizen, can be written using a recursive reference to `citizen`:

```
citizen_or_settled_in_UK (X)  :-
      citizen (X).

citizen_or_settled_in_UK (X)  :-
      settled_in_UK (X).
```

Abandoned infants

The above section 1.-(1) covers one group of people who qualify for citizenship because they are born citizens; indeed it is the one by which most people will be deemed to be citizens by birth. However, it does not cover *everyone* who is born a UK citizen. For example, there are some unfortunate cases where an infant is abandoned at birth. In such a case, how do we know whether or not the infant was actually born in the UK? Or was born after or on the commencement date? Also, as a rule, the parents cannot be determined, and therefore neither parent is definitely known to satisfy the final condition in the definition of the predicate `citizen`, namely:

```
citizen_or_settled_in_UK (Parent)
```

Even though the infant may well satisfy all the necessary conditions to qualify for citizenship under section 1.-(1), this cannot actually be proved. Rather than exclude such an infant from citizenship, the next section of the Act (section 1.-(2)) is designed to deal with this case. It effectively says an abandoned infant is treated as though it had the necessary qualifications; it states that:

> (2)   A new-born infant who, after commencement, is found abandoned in the United Kingdom shall, unless the contrary is shown, be deemed for the purposes of subsection (1):
>   (a) to have been born in the United Kingdom after commencement; and
>   (b) to have been born to a parent who at the time of the birth was a British citizen or settled in the United Kingdom.

Note that in specifying the condition *'unless the contrary is shown'*, this section of the Act is giving the new-born infant the benefit of the doubt, but *only if there is any doubt*. There will be no doubt if the infant is somehow known to fail at least one of the conditions in earlier section 1.-(1) (and is therefore not a citizen). In other words, a person qualifies for British citizenship under section 1.-(2) if:

(i) They were found as a new-born infant abandoned in the UK after commencement.

(ii) It is *not* known that they were not born in the UK after commencement.

(iii) It is *not* known that neither parent was qualified to be a British citizen under section 1.-(1) at time of birth.

With so many negatives around, things can become a little confusing; so let us take it gradually. To qualify under section 1.-(2), a person must satisfy each of the above three conditions. Take the three conditions separately:

(i) This can be expressed in Prolog as:

```
found_abandoned_in_UK (X),
found_on (Date),
after_commencement (Date)
```

(ii) The second condition will fail if either of the following is known:

- X was born outside the UK.
- X was born before the commencement date.

So we could define another predicate which specifies these conditions:

```
born_outside_UK_or_before_commencement (X) :-
     born_in (X, Place),
     not (Place = uk).
```

```
born_outside_UK_or_before_commencement (X) :-
     born_on_date (X, Date),
     not (after_commencement (Date)).
```

in which case condition (ii) above can be expressed as:

```
not (born_outside_UK_or_before_commencement
                                        (X))
```

(iii) If the second condition seemed complicated, try this one. We might attempt to express it in a Prolog-like notation as:

> not (*X was not born to a parent*
> *who qualifies under section 1.1 at time of birth*)

Expressing this in true Prolog turns out to be fraught with problems. In the end, the Imperial College team found that for most practical purposes, the best way of determining if this condition would be satisfied is to query the user. In other words, instead of writing a whole set of Prolog rules which would evaluate the condition, let the user do the work!

More problems

This last of the above three conditions about an abandoned new-born infant raises another problem which at present the predicate citizen cannot handle. It qualifies the citizenship of the parent by talking about them having become a citizen *under section 1.-(1)*, and about them being a citizen *at the time of the infant's birth*. Therefore, in addition to knowing whether someone (in this case the infant's parent) is a citizen, it is necessary to know:

- Under *which section* do they qualify for citizenship?
- Do they qualify for citizenship *on a particular date*?

Thus, there is the concept of a person acquiring citizenship under a particular section, and on a particular date:

> *X acquires citizenship by section S on date D*

which would have to be written (less readably) in Prolog as:

```
acquires_citizenship (X, S, D)
```

Given this, our original predicate citizen must be modified to include also the section and date. A person is qualified for citizenship under a particular section and on a particular date if the date is on or after the date on which they originally acquired citizenship:

```
qualifies_for_citizenship (X, Section, Date) :-
    acquires_citizenship (X, Section, D),
    after_or_on (Date, D).
```

Rewriting sections 1.-(1) and 1.-(2) in this format gives the picture so far:

```
acquires_citizenship (X, section_1_1, Date):-
    born_in (X, uk),
    born_on_date (X, Date),
    after_commencement (Date),
    parent_of (Parent, X),
    citizen_or_settled_in_UK (Parent).

acquires_citizenship (X, section_1_2, Date):-
    found_abandoned_in_UK (X),
    found_on (Date),
    after_commencement (Date),
    not (
    born_outside_UK_or_before_commencement
                                        (X)),
```
not   (*X was not born to a parent who qualifies
        under section 1.1 at time of birth*) .

where this last condition is informally expressed for now, and would have to be replaced by a predicate which queried the user for the answer.

Further complications

It will be fairly obvious by now that defining the complete 73-page Act in every detail is a major task. And we have not even met some of the more tricky points; for instance:

(i) Since a person's parent could have died before the child was born, the parent may not technically be a citizen at the time of the child's birth. Our present formulation could debar the child from citizenship. A special rule needs to be added to cover this case.

(ii) There is a Section 50.-(9) of the Act which specifies that a man is a 'parent' of his legitimate children only. Section 47, however, allows illegitimate children to become legitimate by the subsequent marriage of the parents. In this case, the father becomes the 'parent' some time after the birth of the children. So it is not enough to define simply that a person X is the parent of another person Y, as in the predicate:

```
parent_of (X, Y)
```

Now, we need to be able to check that X is the parent of Y *on a particular date.* This requires a predicate which states (in English) that:

X is the parent of Y on the specified Date

This will be represented in Prolog by a predicate such as:

```
parent_of_on_date (X, Y, Date)
```

Thus, every reference to parents must take the date into account.

(iii) One of the conditions for citizenship given in the Act states that a certain person is a citizen:

' if ... his mother is a citizen
or would have been a citizen had she been male'

It is hard enough for a lawyer to handle this, let alone a Prolog program!

Despite these difficulties, however, the team at Imperial College was able to translate almost all of the Act into Prolog. The resulting Prolog program could be run, and answer queries such as:

Is Fred a British citizen by section S on 1st May 1986?

Given the above problems, this was obviously quite an achievement, both for the Imperial College team, and for Prolog.

7.4   How valid is this approach?

The fact that it has proved possible to formulate a sizeable proportion of a major piece of real law such as the British Nationality Act may have dispelled some of our earlier doubts concerning being over-enthusiastic about using this approach. But in the last analysis, the validity of the approach will have to be judged by legal experts, who know and understand law and the legal process in much greater depth than computer scientists. So what do legal experts think of the Prolog approach?

The answer seems to be: not a lot. Serious legal arguments have been raised against using a Prolog formalisation of the law to replace legal experts. One particularly scathing attack on the work at Imperial College has come recently from Philip Leith, a lecturer in the Department of Jurisprudence, Queen's University Belfast (published in *The Computer Journal*, December 1986). Leith criticises the position of the Imperial College team, as being '...*a dangerous oversimplification*...', and he claims '*it epitomises dangerous anti-democratic procedures*'. He also says that there is a '*difference between the claims of the Imperial College team and "real" law*'.

What particularly seems to worry Leith is that this approach might be adopted in other areas of law, where matters are less clear-cut than in the British Nationality Act. One argument, for instance, is that much of the legal system is based on *case law*, in which previous cases and judgements are used as guide-lines. In this regard, the British Nationality Act is not typical of other laws, because it is relatively new, and there is as yet very little case law to supplement the legislation. In fairness, though, the Imperial team were the first to point this out.

Another factor is that what might seem clear-cut to one court may not be clear-cut to another. Hence the need for Courts of Appeal. When faced with the same evidence, different judges can sometimes come to different conclusions. It is difficult to define precisely terms like '*having reasonable excuse*' or '*being of good character*'. Of course, one could argue that these areas of doubt ought to be clarified, perhaps by attempting to give a Prolog formulation, and that the more formal approach of the Imperial team could help those who actually make laws to be more precise in their legislation.

In retrospect, it is probably true to say that, in attempting to computerise the process of applying the law, the Imperial College team have chosen one of the most difficult applications imaginable. The reasoning process which is called for in making judgements in a court of law is an extremely complex one, and one which requires a judge to undergo decades of training. The fact that two judges can come to different conclusions when faced with the same evidence does not necessarily mean that they have been illogical in applying the law, or that the law has been badly defined. It is more likely to mean that the problem is inherently extremely difficult. For several centuries, parliaments around the world have been striving to find the best definition of what is 'fair', and to enshrine that in the laws which they make. So to expect that a Prolog definition can capture what has been eluding the human race for centuries is a little unreasonable. It is almost inevitable that any Prolog formulation will in some sense miss the mark, and therefore be unfair. This is the fundamental worry. A computer system based on such a Prolog system would have no inbuilt notion of fairness, let alone kindness or mercy. It would have to rely solely on the definition with which it is supplied. This in turn puts a huge responsibility on those who draw up the Prolog definition. It is probably these reasons, rather than a blind fear of technology, which lie behind many people's reluctance to accept computerised judgements in complex legal cases.

And so the argument could go on. Whatever the outcome, however, the idea of applying a formal approach using Prolog in an attempt to clarify a complex real-world problem was a brave and imaginative venture. Even if from a practical point of view it ultimately proves to have been over-ambitious, the same approach can still usefully be applied to many other less complex problems, which are sitting there just waiting to be tackled.

8

An application in medicine

So far all our programs have used *exact* reasoning, where evaluation of a
goal either succeeds or fails. There are no options in between.
Unfortunately, life is not quite as simple as this. Because some problem
areas are so complex, the most that even an expert in such an area could
hope to give is a definite 'maybe'. The subject of this chapter is an
example of a problem of this type — the problem of medical diagnosis.

8.1 Simple medical diagnosis

When faced with a patient who may or may not be suffering from a
particular illness, a doctor cannot usually give a definite and unique
identification of the illness. This does not indicate a lack of ability or
intelligence on the doctor's part. It is more because the only evidence
which a doctor has to go on is what symptoms are observed, and this is
often insufficient to identify the illness uniquely. Several illnesses may
produce similar symptoms, in the earlier stages at least; and some illnesses
do not produce all the symptoms in the early stages. So when working
backwards from the symptoms, a doctor must consider several possibilities. It may be, of course, that some of these possibilities are more likely
than others, and so the result of a diagnosis could well be a list of possible
illnesses, with some indication of how likely each is. For instance, a quick
examination of a patient might result in the following diagnosis:

> *influenza*   *very likely*
> *gastroenteritis*   *possible*
> *meningitis*   *doubtful*

How does a doctor arrive at this sort of conclusion? The process is
certainly a complex one. But a doctor will make considerable use of

established medical knowledge about illnesses, their symptoms, how common each illness is, how significant a symptom is, and so on. All this medical knowledge we can call a *knowledge base*. This knowledge base will generally be fixed from one patient to the next. What *does* alter with a change of patient, however, is the doctor's knowledge of the patient's symptoms. As a patient is examined, the doctor is building up a separate, *local* knowledge base about the patient. As well as these two knowledge bases, there is a third component in the doctor's diagnosis system — a reasoning mechanism. This performs the mental searching of the medical knowledge base, and matches it with the patient's observed symptoms in the local knowledge base. This reasoning mechanism is sometimes called the *inference engine*. Thus the overall structure of the diagnosis system can be viewed as shown below. Some may prefer to group both knowledge bases together into a single knowledge base (thus giving the same structure of an Expert System which was discussed in Chapter 1). However, separating the knowledge base into two gives a little more useful structure.

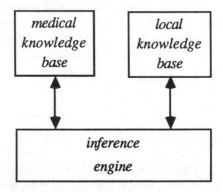

We want to examine each of these three components in rather more detail, with a view to trying eventually to model the behaviour of a doctor by writing a simple Prolog diagnosis program. Realistically, we can only hope to approximate a doctor's performance, since the actual process would be far too complex to program even if we knew exactly how it operated (which we do not). But before attempting to write a Prolog solution to the problem, let us first analyse in more detail the three components which we have identified as being part of even a human diagnosis system. This will be an intermediate description, before we later embark upon the task of expressing the solution in Prolog.

The local knowledge base

This is relatively straightforward, if all it has to hold are the symptoms the patient is presently displaying. When the inference engine is performing the diagnosis, and needs to know what symptoms the patient has, it will consult this local knowledge base. It will do this effectively by asking the question:

> *Does the patient have a particular symptom?*

For instance, it may be necessary to ask:

> *Does the patient have a runny nose?*

We assume for simplicity that the answer to such a question will be a straight yes or no.

The medical knowledge base

The medical knowledge base holds all the necessary information about each illness and its various symptoms. But how should this information be structured and quantified?

As a starting point, the information held for each illness might just be a list of the expected symptoms. An illness would then be described in the knowledge base by a description which has two parts — the name of the illness, and a list of symptoms. Let us write this in the form of a Prolog predicate:

> `illness` (*name of illness, list of symptoms for this illness*) .

For instance, a rather simple knowledge base might contain the illness descriptions:

> `illness (influenza,`   *symptoms of influenza*) .
> `illness (meningitis,`   *symptoms of meningitis*) .
> `illness (measles,`   *symptoms of measles*) .
> `illness (gastroenteritis,`   *symptoms of gastroenteritis*) .

To describe a symptom, we will just give each symptom a name, like *temperature*, or *nausea*. But later on we will have to associate more information with a symptom, so a symptom will become a structured object. So let us begin now with a description of a symptom as a structured object of the form:

> `symptom`(*name of symptom*)

Using this description, the symptoms for each of the diseases in the knowledge base can be added. The following is a rather simplistic description of our state of knowledge about the four illnesses in the knowledge base:

```
illness (influenza,
              [symptom(runny_nose),
               symptom(temperature)]).

illness (meningitis,
              [symptom(headache),
               symptom(temperature),
               symptom(nausea)]).

illness (measles,
              [symptom(spots)]).

illness (gastroenteritis,
              [symptom(nausea),
               symptom(temperature)]).
```

It would now be possible to go through each illness description in turn, see if the patient has the expected symptoms, and hence arrive at a conclusion about whether the illness is a possibility. For instance, if the patient has a headache, a temperature, and is feeling sick, we might diagnose the patient as having either meningitis or gastroenteritis. However, this makes no allowance for the fact that some illnesses are more common than others, and are therefore more likely to be observed. For instance, a patient with a temperature is more likely to be suffering from gastroenteritis than from meningitis, since one is a more common illness than the other. It makes sense, therefore, to extend the information held for each illness by including a measure of how common or likely it is. The most convenient way to do this is to specify its *probability*.

Probability

The *probability* of something happening or being true is an estimate in the form of a number of how likely that thing is. Usually this number is given in the range 0.0 to 1.0. A probability of 0.0 means there is no chance of it at all — it's reckoned to be impossible. A probability of 1.0 means it is reckoned to be an absolute certainty. In between, the probability gives an estimate of how likely it is. For instance, if there is a fifty–fifty chance, the probability is 0.5. But because standard Prolog does not let us write numbers which are not whole numbers, what we will do is represent the probability as a *percentage* — as a whole number between 0 and 100. Then, a probability of 100% will mean absolute certainty; 50% means there is a fifty–fifty chance; 10% means there is a one in ten chance; and 0% means it is reckoned to be impossible. This may result in a little loss of accuracy, since parts of a percent are not allowed (as in 1.5%). But for our purposes, this is not crucial.

For instance, if it is estimated that one person in ten of those who consult a doctor is suffering from influenza, then the probability of influenza is one in ten, or 10%. This probability is the chance that any patient visiting a doctor, selected at random from all those who consult the doctor, will have influenza, without considering any symptoms.

Returning now to the problem of stating how common each illness is, what we need to do is to include the probability of the illness as part of the illness description which we have been developing to represent the knowledge base. Incorporating this probability into an illness description gives a third item to be held in each description. The format of an illness description consequently becomes:

> illness (*name, initial probability,* [*... list of symptoms ...*]) .

where *initial probability* is the chance that any patient who comes to consult the doctor will have the named illness. This might give us the following knowledge base:

```
illness (influenza, 10,
                  [symptom(runny_nose),
                   symptom(temperature)]).

illness (meningitis, 1,
                  [symptom(headache),
                   symptom(temperature),
                   symptom(nausea)]).

illness (measles, 5,
                  [symptom(spots)]).

illness (gastroenteritis, 6,
                  [symptom(nausea),
                   symptom(temperature)]).
```

The probability figures quoted here (10%, 1%, 5% and 6%) imply that, from a random sample of 100 people who consult the doctor, we would expect:

> 10 to be suffering from influenza
> 1 to be suffering from meningitis
> 5 to be suffering from measles
> 6 to be suffering from gastroenteritis

These probabilities are of course extremely dubious, and would need to be supplied by a medical expert on the basis of medical experience of the illnesses.

Symptom description

Even the description above does not give enough information to enable us to arrive at a reliable conclusion. There are two main reasons for this. If we are considering the likelihood of the patient having a particular illness, then:

(i) A patient can have an illness without necessarily showing all the symptoms of that illness, perhaps because the symptoms have not all developed yet.

(ii) A patient can have some of the symptoms of an illness, but not actually have that illness. This could be because the symptoms result from a different illness, which has some symptoms in common.

Let us examine each of these problems in turn.

(i) Illness without the symptom

When someone has an illness, they may not necessarily display all the expected symptoms. Some symptoms of an illness may be more likely to appear than others. Some may be definitely expected, so it is very significant if they are not observed; with others, it may not be that significant if they are not present. So in our illness description, each symptom will need to be *weighted* in proportion to how likely it is to be observed in someone with the illness. The *weight factor* is included for every symptom in the list. A symptom with a high weight factor is very likely to be observed; so if it is not present then this is quite significant. On the other hand, a symptom with a low weight factor is not so commonly displayed, so it will not be that significant if it is not observed. To accommodate this information, the description of a symptom needs to be extended to include this weight factor:

```
symptom (name, weight factor)
```

For instance:

```
illness (influenza,  10,
                [symptom(runny_nose,   90),
                 symptom(temperature, 100)]).
```

This states that:

- 90% of people who have influenza have a runny nose. So one in ten 'flu victims for some reason has a nose which does not run. This is a case of someone having the illness but not the symptom.
- 100% of people who have influenza have a temperature. So if you do not have a temperature, you do not have 'flu.

(ii) Symptom without the illness

A symptom is rarely unique to a single illness. One which is common to several illnesses may not be as helpful as one which is unique to a particular illness. So some symptoms of an illness will be more telling than others. Again, therefore, each symptom of an illness will have to be *weighted* to give an indication of its 'uniqueness'. A symptom which is relatively common will tell us less than one which is comparatively rare. In our illness description below, we have chosen the weight factor to be the probability that the symptom *results from some other illness*, and not the one under consideration. The description of a symptom therefore needs to be extended yet again to include this information:

symptom (*name, weight factor 1, weight factor 2*)

The first weight factor is the one we have already considered. If this symptom is included in the list of symptoms of a particular illness, then:

- *weight factor 1* is the probability that the symptom will be observed in someone who *has* this illness. This weight factor will from now on be referred to as P_y (*P* for probability, and *y* for yes);
- *weight factor 2* is the probability that the symptom will be observed in someone who does *not* have this illness (but presumably has some other illness of which this is a symptom). This weight factor will from now on be referred to as P_n (*P* for probability, *n* for no).

Given suitable figures from a medical expert, our updated description of influenza might now look like:

```
illness (influenza,   10,
          [symptom(runny_nose,   90,   40),
           symptom(temperature,  100,  25)]).
```

This additional information implies, for instance, that 40% of patients who have a runny nose have it for some reason other than influenza. Likewise, one person in four (25%) of patients who have a temperature have it for some reason other than influenza. If these statistics were available for all the illnesses in the knowledge base, our knowledge base could at last be completed. The extended knowledge base for the previous example set of illnesses is shown below. Again, the medical basis for the figures is rather dubious.

```
illness (influenza,   10,
          [symptom(runny_nose,   90,   40),
           symptom(temperature,  100,  25)]).

illness (meningitis,   1,
          [symptom(headache,      98,   90),
           symptom(temperature,   95,   85),
           symptom(nausea,        85,   80)]).

illness (measles,   5,
          [symptom(spots,         90,   5)]).
```

```
illness (gastroenteritis,  6,
            [symptom(nausea,        70,   75),
            symptom(temperature, 80,   90)]).
```

Given a knowledge base like this, and information in the local knowledge base about the patient's observed symptoms, we will now consider in more detail the reasoning behind a doctor's diagnosis, carried out by what has been called the inference engine. This requires the diagnostic process to be examined in more detail.

8.2   The diagnostic process

To try to analyse the process of diagnosis which a doctor carries out, we will trace an example session in slow motion. To help break down the process further, the symptoms will be fed to the doctor one at a time, rather than all at once.

The scenario is this: one Monday morning, the doctor receives a telephone call from Mrs Robinson, whose son Jimmy claims he has 'flu, and therefore unfortunately cannot go to school.

Mrs R.: *Do you think Jimmy has 'flu, doctor?*

Pause at this point. What are the chances that Jimmy does have influenza, given no evidence yet? Treating Jimmy as a random sample from those who consult a doctor, and using our knowledge base above, the doctor could reply straightaway:

There's a chance of about one in ten, Mrs Robinson.

This information comes from the initial probability of someone who consults a doctor having influenza (10%). Obviously, though, the doctor ought to take any symptoms into account before giving a considered opinion, rather than giving an answer immediately. From the knowledge held about influenza, the first symptom expected is a runny nose. So the doctor first asks:

Does Jimmy have a runny nose?

Depending on the answer to this question, the doctor's mental estimate of the probability of influenza will be updated from its present value of 10%, either up or down. If the answer is 'yes', the probability will increase by a certain amount; if it is 'no', we would expect it to decrease somewhat. The precise amount of the variation resulting from this new information will be considered later. But in general, if it is a significant symptom, the variation will be more than for a less significant symptom. Thus the variation will depend on the two weighting factors associated with the symptom. Let us suppose that Mrs Robinson reports that Jimmy does indeed have a runny nose; on the basis of this, let us say the doctor makes an informed guess and estimates that the chance of influenza has now doubled, and is one in five (20%).

The knowledge base now indicates that the next question to ask is:

Does Jimmy have a temperature?

Again, if Mrs Robinson investigates, and returns the answer 'yes', the doctor will update the current probability from 20% to, say, 50% (one in two). At this point, with all expected symptoms in the illness description in the knowledge base now considered, the doctor could reply:

There's a fifty–fifty chance that Jimmy has 'flu.

If instead the answer had been 'no', what would the new probability be? The knowledge base indicates that *all* 'flu victims have a temperature, since the P_y weight factor is 100. Therefore, the doctor can in these circumstances say unequivocally that there is no chance of Jimmy having influenza.

Thus, the process of estimating how likely it is that a patient has a given illness is a repetitive one, beginning with an initial estimate and gradually working towards a more accurate answer. More systematically, the diagnostic process is as follows:

- Start with the initial probability.
- Consider the symptoms one at a time.
- For each symptom, update the current probability, taking into account:
    - whether or not the patient has the symptom;
    - the weight factors P_y and P_n.

The awkward stage of this process is clearly updating the probability in the light of each piece of new evidence. This is the heart of the *inference engine*. In particular, what should the adjustment be, numerically? How was the sequence of revised estimates (20%, then 50%) arrived at? Was it pure guess-work? Fortunately, an approach to this problem has been around for some time, and seems to give reasonable results. We will use the method developed by Bayes.

Bayes' Theorem

The problem of drawing an inference in the light of some new piece of evidence was studied in some depth by the Reverend Bayes, an eighteenth century English vicar. He developed a formula for calculating the new probability of some theory being true, given the old probability plus some new piece of evidence. We will use this formula, known as Bayes' Theorem, for the basic inference step in the diagnostic process.

Suppose we have a theory that the patient has a particular illness. This theory might be that the patient has influenza. Also suppose that the probability of this theory being true is currently estimated to be *p* percent. We want to calculate an updated estimate *p*' given a piece of new evidence (a symptom) with weights P_y and P_n as defined previously. Bayes' Theorem gives a formula for calculating this updated estimate, and states that:

$$p' = \frac{100 * P_y * p}{P_y * p + P_n (100-p)}$$

Reviewing the above diagnosis session, at the very start the first value of *p* is the 'initial' probability of influenza, 10%. Given the first piece of new evidence — a runny nose (for which $P_y = 90$ and $P_n = 40$) — the doctor's revised estimate can be modelled using the above formula:

$$p' = \frac{100 * 90 * 10}{90 * 10 + 40 (100 - 10)} = 20$$

Thus, after considering a single piece of evidence, the estimate of the probability has gone up from 10% to 20%, using Bayes' Theorem. This revised estimate now becomes our current estimate of the probability.

For the next step, we are given a second piece of evidence — a temperature. For this piece of evidence, $P_y = 100$ and $P_n = 25$. We can use Bayes' formula again; but this time we substitute back in the revised estimate (*p*', or 20) as the new value of *p*:

$$p' = \frac{100 * 100 * 20}{100 * 20 + 25 (100 - 20)} = 50$$

So considering this second piece of evidence has raised the estimate of the probability again, from 20% to 50%. This means there is now a fifty–fifty chance of influenza. If there was more evidence to be considered, we could obviously keep on repeating this process, using the formula over and over again, and substituting back in again the last value we had calculated, until all the expected symptoms in the knowledge base have been considered. The final value of *p*' is then the resulting probability.

Bayes' Theorem above updates the probability on the basis of a new symptom which *is* observed. But what if the patient does *not* have the expected symptom? This is surely significant, and should cause the estimate to be revised, downwards. In this case, the formula to be used is similar, except that P_y is replaced by $(100 - P_y)$, and P_n by $(100 - P_n)$:

$$p' = \frac{100 * (100 - P_y) * p}{(100 - P_y) * p + (100 - P_n) (100 - p)}$$

For instance, if when considering the first symptom, the patient was discovered *not* to have a runny nose, then we use this second formula (with the initial estimate of 10%) to give:

$$p' = \frac{100 * (100 - 90) * 10}{(100 - 90) * 10 \; + \; (100 - 40) * (100 - 10)}$$

$$= 2 \quad \text{(approximately)}$$

Thus, *not* observing a symptom which was expected has reduced the estimated probability from 10% to just 2%. Note also that if $P_y = 100$ and the symptom is *not* present, then p' always works out to be 0. This was the case for temperature. This is exactly what we would expect, since a probability of 0 means the patient definitely does not have the illness.

Gathering all this together, the basic inference step can be put more precisely as follows:

- Given an expected symptom with weights P_y and P_n, and a current probability p, then:

  - if the patient *has* the symptom, then:

$$new \; probability = \frac{100 * P_y * p}{P_y * p + P_n (100 - p)}$$

  - if the patient does *not* have the symptom, then:

$$new \; probability = \frac{100 * (100 - P_y) * p}{(100 - P_y) * p + (100 - P_n)(100 - p)}$$

Given a decent knowledge base and a pocket calculator, it would now be possible to make an attempt at copying the diagnostic process, even if we were not a trained doctor. In fact, this process can be programmed relatively simply in Prolog, which is exactly what is now going to be done.

8.3 Programming the system

Recall that we have been viewing the doctor's mind as having three components:

- *A medical knowledge base*
        (of illnesses, expected symptoms, and so on).
- *A local knowledge base*
        (the patient's observed symptoms).
- *An inference engine*, or reasoning ability.

Let us consider how each of these can be represented in Prolog. We will begin with the most straightforward of the three components: the local knowledge base.

The local knowledge base

This has to hold the information on the current patient, namely which symptoms have been observed. The fact that a particular symptom has been observed can be included in the program by defining it by a predicate:

```
observed (Symptom).
```

For instance, the local knowledge base held for a patient with a runny nose and a temperature would be:

```
observed (runny_nose).
observed (temperature).
```

These facts would need to be added to the program after an examination of the patient. Thereafter, the symptoms of the current patient could, if required, be displayed by the query:

```
?-observed (Symptom).
```

which for the above patient would produce the following response, if all solutions were requested:

```
Symptom = runny_nose;
Symptom = temperature;
no
```

The medical knowledge base

So far, the medical knowledge base has been represented by a set of definitions of illness descriptions using the predicate:

```
illness (name, initial probability, [...list of symptoms... ]).
```

For instance:

```
illness (influenza,  10,
              [symptom(runny_nose,  90,   40),
               symptom(temperature, 100,  25)]).
```

A complete illness description in this format states all that is known about the illness (for our diagnostic purposes, at any rate). Defining a new rule for every illness gives the complete knowledge base. We have already seen an example of a particularly simple knowledge base defined in this way:

```
illness (influenza,  10,
              [symptom(runny_nose,  90,   40),
               symptom(temperature, 100,  25)]).
```

```
illness (meningitis,  1,
            [symptom(headache,     98,  90),
             symptom(temperature, 95,  85),
             symptom(nausea,       85,  80)]).

illness (measles,  5,
            [symptom(spots,        90,  5)]).

illness (gastroenteritis,  6,
            [symptom(nausea,       70,  75),
             symptom(temperature, 80,  90)]).
```

These facts can be accessed and queried in the usual way. Consider the following example queries:

(i) *What is the initial probability of meningitis?*

```
?-illness (meningitis, Probability, _).
```

This would produce the answer:

```
Probability = 1
```

(ii) *Which illnesses have an initial probability of more than one in ten?*

```
?-illness (Illness, Probability, _),
   Probability > 10.
```

(iii) *Which illnesses have nausea as a symptom?* Assuming the availability of a predicate contains to test for membership of a list (described in Chapter 4), this could be expressed as:

```
?-illness (Illness, _, Symptom_list),
   contains (Symptom_list,
             symptom(nausea, _, _)).
```

Thus, the first two components of the system — the local and medical knowledge bases — have been relatively simple to represent in Prolog. This leaves the inference engine section, which is not quite as easy, but is still not very difficult.

The inference engine

The inference engine's task is to match the expected symptoms of the illnesses in the knowledge base with the patient's actual symptoms, and produce a list of (reasonably) possible illnesses, together with the likelihood of each. The fact that the current patient could have an illness with a certain probability can be defined by the predicate:

```
patient_could_have (Illness, Probability)
```

This relation states that the patient could have an Illness with a (reasonable) Probability. For a typical patient, if the following query is used to find all reasonable diagnoses given the patient's symptoms:

```
?-patient_could_have (Illness, Probability).
```

then this might produce the following response:

```
Illness = influenza
Probability = 50;
Illness = meningitis
Probability = 10;
Illness = gastroenteritis
Probability = 15;
no
```

Consider now how this predicate should be defined. There are three conditions which need to be satisfied:

- `Illness` must be an illness in the medical knowledge base.
- The chance of the patient having `Illness` is `Probability`.
- `Probability` must indicate a reasonable chance.

Expressing these conditions in Prolog gives the following attempt at a definition of the relation `patient_could_have`:

```
patient_could_have (Illness, Probability) :-
      illness (Illness, _, _),
      probability (Illness, Probability),
      reasonable (Probability).
```

The predicate `reasonable` should eliminate possible illnesses which turn out to have a very low probability. A lower threshold value needs to be chosen as a cut-off value. The selection of this value would require a few trials; but let us say for now that anything below 10% is not worth considering:

```
reasonable (Probability) :- Probability >= 10.
```

This leaves only the second condition, which is really the core of the diagnosis problem:

```
probability (Illness, Probability)
```

Recall that our model of the diagnostic process is a repetitive process, which considers the expected symptoms one at a time, and maintains a probability which is updated during each step. Therefore, at any intermediate stage in this process, we have two items of information:

- The current probability.
- A list of symptoms which have still to be considered.

On the basis of these, a third value has to be calculated, namely the new probability. This new probability will be calculated by updating the current probability in the light of the list of symptoms still to be considered. We will define the relationship between these three objects by a predicate:

```
new_probability (P_current,
                 Symptom_list,
                 P_new)
```

where:

`P_current`	is the current probability;
`Symptom_list`	is the list of symptoms still to be considered;
`P_new`	will be the new probability, arrived at by considering the symptoms in the list `Symptom_list`.

Once this predicate has been defined, it can be used in the definition of the predicate `probability` which appears in the above definition of `patient_could_have`. For, at the very start, before any symptoms have been taken into account, the current probability is just the initial probability, and the list of remaining symptoms is the original list of symptoms in the knowledge base. Thus, the definition of `probability` is quite straightforward:

```
probability (Illness, Probability) :-
     illness (Illness, P_current,
                       Symptom_list),
     new_probability (P_current,
                      Symptom_list,
                      Probability).
```

Now consider how we might define `new_probability`. It has to process the list of symptom descriptors, one at a time, until the list is empty. In fact, it is possible that the list of symptoms *is* empty to start with, in which case it is simple to define this case of the relation `new_probability`:

```
new_probability (P, [], P).
```

This states that if there are no more symptoms, then our estimate of the probability does not change; therefore the new probability is the same as the old probability.

However, it is more likely that there will be at least one symptom still to be considered. In this case, the non-empty list of symptoms will be decomposed into the first symptom plus the remainder list:

```
new_probability (P_current,
                 [Symptom| Tail],
                 P_new) :- ...
```

where Symptom will be the descriptor for the next expected symptom. Following the usual list processing pattern, the list of symptoms will be considered in two stages:

(i) The first symptom in the list will be considered; starting with the initial probability P_current, a calculation based on Bayes' Theorem will give us the first updated estimate of the probability, called P_updated, say.

(ii) Having considered one symptom and obtained an updated probability, we are left with another list of symptoms to be considered — the list Tail. This list will be processed in exactly the same way, by a recursive use of the predicate new_probability. This second stage begins with a probability estimate of P_updated, and the resulting probability is the answer we are looking for, called P_new. Expressing this in Prolog gives the following:

```
new_probability (P_current,
             [Symptom| Tail], P_new) :-
      update (P_current, Symptom, P_updated),
      new_probability (P_updated,
                       Tail, P_new).
```

Only the predicate update needs to be defined now:

```
update (P_current, Symptom, P_updated)
```

Updating the probability P_current in the light of a new symptom descriptor Symptom will use Bayes' Theorem, in exactly the same way as before. There are two problems to be addressed:

(i) The weight factors P_y and P_n have to be extracted from the symptom descriptor Symptom.

(ii) The actual calculation which uses these weight factors according to Bayes' formula has to be performed.

Let us take the second of these two problems first. Recall that Bayes' formula calculated a new probability p' on the basis of the current probability p and the two weight factors P_y and P_n, as follows:

$$p' = \frac{100 * P_y * p}{P_y * p + P_n (100 - p)}$$

We will define a predicate which specifies the relationship between these four quantities, and performs the calculation. Using the variable names P, Pdash, Py and Pn to represent p, p', P_y and P_n, respectively, this predicate can be defined as follows:

```
bayes (P, Py, Pn, Pdash) :-
    Top is 100 * Py * P,
    Bottom is (Py * P) + (Pn * (100 - P)),
    Pdash is Top / Bottom.
```

The other problem mentioned above is that of extracting the weight factors P_y and P_n from the symptom descriptor which is the second argument in the predicate update. This is straightforward, since in the heading of the predicate, the object can be decomposed to give names to each of the components, as shown:

```
update (P_current,
        symptom (Symptom_name, Py, Pn),
        P_new)
```

Now consider the definition of update. This performs the basic inference step outlined previously. Recall that there were two cases to be taken into account when considering how the probability should vary in the light of an expected symptom:

- The symptom *is* observed. In this case, Bayes' formula is used directly.
- The symptom is *not* observed. In this case, the formula to be used is Bayes' formula with P_y replaced by $(100 - P_y)$, and P_n replaced by $(100 - P_n)$.

Writing these alternative cases as two separate rules gives the following definition of update:

```
update (P_current,
        symptom(Symptom_name, Py, Pn),
        P_new) :-
    observed (Symptom_name),
    bayes (P_current, Py, Pn, P_new).

update (P_current,
        symptom(Symptom_name, Py, Pn),
        P_new) :-
    not (observed (Symptom_name)),
    P1 is 100 - Py,
    P2 is 100 - Pn,
    bayes (P_current, P1, P2, P_new).
```

The program below is the complete Prolog program for diagnosis, including the example knowledge base and typical patient details. Comments are included in curly brackets.

```
{ The medical knowledge base ... }

illness (influenza, 10,
            [symptom(runny_nose,    90,    40),
             symptom(temperature,  100,    25)]).

illness (meningitis, 1,
            [symptom(headache,      98,    90),
             symptom(temperature,   95,    85),
             symptom(nausea,        85,    80)]).

illness (measles, 5,
            [symptom(spots,         90,     5)]).

illness (gastroenteritis, 6,
            [symptom(nausea,        70,    75),
             symptom(temperature,   80,    90)]).


{ The local knowledge base ... }

observed (runny_nose).
observed (temperature).


{ The inference engine ... }

patient_could_have (Illness, Probability) :-
    illness (Illness, _, _),
    probability (Illness, Probability),
    reasonable (Probability).

reasonable (Probability) :- Probability >= 10.


probability (Illness, Probability) :-
    illness (Illness,
                P_current, Symptom_list),
        new_probability (P_current,
                    Symptom_list,
                    Probability).

new_probability (P, [], P).
```

```
new_probability (P_current,
                 [Symptom| Tail], P_new) :-
     update (P_current, Symptom, P_updated),
     new_probability (P_updated, Tail, P_new).

update (P_current,
        symptom(Symptom_name, Py, Pn),
        P_new) :-
     observed (Symptom_name),
     bayes (P_current, Py, Pn, P_new).

update (P_current,
        symptom(Symptom_name, Py, Pn),
        P_new) :-
     not (observed (Symptom_name)),
     P1 is 100 - Py,
     P2 is 100 - Pn,
     bayes (P_current, P1, P2, P_new).

bayes (P, Py, Pn, Pdash) :-
     Top is 100 * Py * P,
     Bottom is (Py * P) + (Pn * (100 - P)),
     Pdash is Top / Bottom.
```

8.4   Operating the system

As it stands, our diagnosis system would not last long in the real world,
mainly because it has a poor medical knowledge base. This could be
remedied, though, with sound medical statistics and a full range of illnesses
and symptoms. We will now consider how such a system would be
operated in practice. Given a more realistic knowledge base, the situation
in which we might envisage such a program being used need not
necessarily involve an actual trained doctor. An untrained operator could
use the system, perhaps for an initial screening of patients. With a little
modification, it might even be left for the patient to operate, giving an
interactive medical advice system.

When a new patient comes along, the program will typically still have
rules defining the symptoms of the previous patient. To clear out the local
knowledge base in preparation for building a new one, any existing
definitions of the predicate observed must be deleted. The Prolog
system which is being used for the program will probably provide editing
operations for deleting and inserting rules; but in any case the built-in
predicates retract and assertz can be used to delete and add new
facts to the program. All existing definitions of observed could be
deleted by asking for all solutions to the query:

```
?-retract (observed(_)).
```

Having done this, each observed symptom of the new patient can be added to the program, in the same way that any rule is added to a program. Again, the system's built-in editing facilities could be used to add rules such as:

```
observed (headache).
observed (nausea).
```

Finally, the actual diagnosis is performed by entering the query:

```
?-patient_could_have (Illness, Probability).
```

Note that a user does not need to be aware of the internal workings of the system, or of all the other predicates which make up the program. Those features of the system which the user needs to see constitute what is called the *user interface*. At present, the user interface of our diagnosis system has a number of shortcomings:

 (i) The user may forget to delete the symptoms of the previous user, or may do it incorrectly. This would cause the system to give wrong answers to the diagnosis query. The worst of it is, the user would not know the answers were wrong.

 (ii) The user could accidently delete part or all of the program when retracting the symptoms of the previous patient.

(iii) Care needs to be taken to enter *all* the symptoms.

(iv) The query above which effectively asks for the diagnosis leaves scope for the user to make a mistake. The user could easily type a lower case letter instead of an upper case one at the start of Illness, or make some other similar mistake. Ideally, a user should merely have to press a single button. This would also be safer.

   As a general rule, assume that if anything could possibly go wrong, then it will. No matter how stupid, how unlikely or how far-fetched the circumstances might appear, never think '*Oh that would never happen. No user would ever do that*'. Some user, somewhere, definitely will. Programs in the real world need to be protected from users, and need to be as convenient and easy to use as possible.

 (v) The list of possible illnesses which appears is not in the order we would want. Possible illnesses will at present be given in the order in which their details are held in the knowledge base, perhaps as follows:

```
Illness = influenza
Probability = 10;
Illness = meningitis
```

```
Probability = 18;
Illness = measles
Probability = 60;
no
```

We would probably prefer the results to appear in decreasing order of likelihood.

(vi) A user may not understand the significance of being told, say, that the probability of meningitis is 18. Should the patient be concerned by this? It would be much better if the calculated probability could first be converted into terms like *very likely* or *possible* or *doubtful* before presenting the answers to the user. For instance, we might try the following ranges:

80 to 100	means	*very likely*
60 to 79	means	*quite likely*
30 to 59	means	*possible*
10 to 29	means	*doubtful*

(Anything below 10 is already considered unreasonable.)

Clearly there is scope for improvement in this user interface aspect of our program, to make it more idiot-proof, more convenient to use, and generally more user-friendly. These issues, though, form a whole subject in themselves, sometimes called Man–Machine Interfaces (MMI) or Human–Computer Interaction (HCI). Fascinating though this subject is, it is unfortunately beyond the scope of this particular book.

Relying on the system

Even if our system was given a realistic knowledge base and was modified to have an excellent user interface, there is one final point which ought to be borne in mind. It would be rather dangerous to allow a computerised diagnosis system like this to be used instead of a doctor, even as a screening device, so that a patient does not get to see the doctor personally. There are at least two reasons for this:

(i) Observing the patient's symptoms is a very skilled job, and can sometimes be the most crucial part of the diagnostic process. Often what distinguishes a good doctor from the rest is the ability to recognise as significant something which a less observant person would miss. This process cannot safely be automated, and cannot even safely be entrusted to an untrained or partially trained assistant.

(ii) Who is legally liable for an incorrect diagnosis? If a doctor through negligence fails to diagnose a serious illness, perhaps resulting in the death of a patient, then the doctor could face prosecution and be sued for a vast sum in compensation. Nowadays, many doctors have to insure themselves against this happening. But with a computerised diagnosis system, who would be legally liable in the event of a serious misdiagnosis? If the law permitted the use of such a system instead of seeing a doctor personally, then strictly speaking it would be the firm who provides the computer system who would be liable. But no sensible insurance firm would insure a computerised diagnosis system against charges of negligence or incompetence. There have already been cases where computer firms have found it impossible to get insurance for their products. This is becoming a major problem for computer system suppliers, since in general it is impossible to guarantee the correct operation of a complex computer system.

9

Expert systems

In the course of the last two example programs, in law and in medical diagnosis, an idea has steadily been developing. This is the idea of using a computer system in the same way that we might use a human expert — as someone to be consulted and to give us sound, reasonable advice based on specialist knowledge and experience. In the law application, for instance, we wondered about the possibility of having a system which could answer our queries about various points of law, in the same way that we might consult a legal expert. The medical diagnosis system took this idea a step further, in that it not only advised what illnesses were possible, but it was also able to handle differing degrees of certainty (or uncertainty). Using a proper system like this would not be unlike having one's own personal medical adviser or expert, who could be consulted for advice which we assume is based on sound medical knowledge and experience. Of course, our medical diagnosis program as it stands has a long way to go before it reaches the point where it would be safe to let it loose on an unsuspecting public. But it does nevertheless contain the seeds of the idea behind a fairly recent class of programs which have similar general aims. These programs have become known as *Expert Systems*. The aim of an expert system is that it can be used and relied upon in more or less the same way as a human expert or consultant. Expert systems are very trendy nowadays, and also big business. So it will be useful to conclude this book by considering what they are, and explaining some of the associated jargon which often obscures their simplicity.

Somehow, when we hear the word *expert*, we immediately think of someone who is especially smart, and among the cleverest in their subject. This is not quite the meaning of the term in the context of expert systems — it is rather the idea of being a *specialist*, and someone who has a *restricted* area of knowledge or expertise. For instance, try asking a doctor to change the spark plugs in a car. Although a doctor may be an expert in diagnosing and treating faults in one type of complex machinery (the human body), when faced with a different type of machine outside his or her practical experience, the same expert can appear very stupid. It is tempting to say that a specialist or expert is not so much someone who knows a lot about their own subject, but rather someone who knows absolutely nothing about any other subject. So rather than give the impression that expert systems are smarter than other systems, perhaps they should have been called *Specialist Systems*. Restricting the area of application of a system like this to a rather specialised area has made these systems easier to construct. Attempts to build all-singing, all-dancing systems which can be expert in any field have, generally speaking, come to nothing.

To understand what is required of an expert system, let us take as a starting point our medical diagnosis program, hold it up as a personal medical adviser, and see how it fares. The practical shortcomings which become apparent will point out which areas need to be strengthened and extended to produce a real expert system.

9.1   The diagnosis program as a medical expert

Given a proper medical knowledge base, our diagnosis program will certainly deliver results and give diagnoses. But would you trust it? Would you even pay much attention to it? If not, then the system has failed. As it stands, the signs are not promising. Even with a very user-friendly interface, even if it could be proved that the reasoning mechanism is perfectly sound, and that Bayes' Theorem gives highly reliable results, users could well still be wary of accepting the system. This is partly because the system lacks two important features of human experts.

Point 1

No-one trusts a medical expert who does not keep up-to-date with the latest advances in medical knowledge. Put more technically, we expect that an expert's knowledge base will never be totally complete, but will be updated with more knowledge during the lifetime of the expert. What this means for our diagnosis program is that it needs a mechanism for updating the medical knowledge base section — perhaps adding details of a new illness, or modifying some of the details of an illness already in the knowledge base. This new information would be supplied by real, human experts working in the same field. This 'continuing education' process, whereby more knowledge is acquired by the program, is called *knowledge acquisition*. Our program would benefit from a section to handle the input and modification of information already in the knowledge base. At present, the program has no special code for this; all we have is the usual set of Prolog editing commands for modifying parts of a Prolog program. But this is hardly a very user-friendly interface.

Point 2

Whenever we are not convinced by a specialist's advice, in practice we might often ask '*How did you arrive at that conclusion?*' Usually a word of explanation is enough to reassure us that the advice is actually sound, and not a guess, or not based on false premises. The ability to explain one's reasoning and conclusions is a key factor in retaining the confidence of the user. Or rather, an *inability* to explain one's reasoning can arouse suspicion and distrust. This applies both to a human expert and to an automated expert. Therefore, it is vital in practice that the user interface includes a section for explaining the system's reasoning. This is called an *explanatory facility*. A user should be able to follow the system's train of thought by asking, for instance:

> *How did you arrive at that conclusion?*

Or, if the system queries the user for a particular piece of information, the user may want to know why it is required:

> *Why did you ask that question?*

At present, our Prolog diagnosis program has no explanation facility. There is a Prolog *trace* or *spy* facility, which was mentioned earlier in section 5.2. This gives a trace of the reasoning process as it occurs, but this is no substitute for a proper explanation.

These two factors would tend to undermine a user's confidence in our diagnosis program over a period of time. There is also a third problem with the system which would quickly render it obsolete. This is not so much a question of user confidence, as of usability.

Point 3

In our diagnosis program, it has been assumed that all the patient's observed symptoms are added to the program by defining a set of facts using the predicate *observed*. This is assumed to have been done *before* a diagnosis query is ever asked. This might not seem very difficult; but to ensure that no symptom is overlooked, presumably the user must go through some sort of check-list of symptoms, considering questions such as:

> *Does the patient have a temperature?*
> *(If so, define a new fact in the program).*

or

> *Does the patient have a runny nose?*
> *(If so, define a new fact in the program).*

This check-list is assumed at present to exist on paper, and to be followed dutifully by the operator of the system. But an improvement would be for the system itself to hold the check-list; it could then also ask the questions at the start of each session with a new patient. The section of program responsible for this process is really a second *knowledge acquisition* section, though the knowledge will be acquired from a different source. This source will be the user, rather than the expert. In effect, we recognise that the system really has *two* users — the expert, and the 'actual' user. Each has its own corresponding knowledge base and its own acquisition section.

This may seem to have improved matters a bit. But think what will happen now. The program must ask the user about *every* symptom which could possibly occur. Given a full medical knowledge base, this means that a patient who only has influenza will still be forced to answer questions like:

> *Does the patient have pupils that dilate?*
> *Does the patient have ingrown toe nails?*

and possibly even more gruesome details. Very soon, a user would get fed up with this, and stop using the system. Obviously, what we would want is for the system to ask for a piece of information only if it has grounds for suspicion that the answer will be significant. This would actually require major structural alterations to the program, in two areas:

(i) the predicate `observed` must be replaced with a rule which usually interrogates the user interactively. Instead of looking for a definition of, say:

```
observed (runny_nose)
```

as a simple fact, the system should ask the user only when it needs to know whether the patient has a runny nose, and read the answer. It would also need to record the answer in the program, so that the same question is not asked twice. This is the technique of querying the user, and updating the program dynamically, which was discussed previously in Chapter 5 (section 5.4).

(ii) The system should try to avoid asking about symptoms which are not ultimately going to be relevant. This will involve calling off the process of considering an illness as soon as it becomes clear that it is not a likely contender. This decision is fairly tricky, and requires a rather more sophisticated inference engine than our program possesses at present.

A revised model

By now, our original diagnosis program may not seem quite as impressive as first impressions might have suggested. Nevertheless, if the three points mentioned above were tackled seriously, we would end up with a fairly useful little system, which would be much more likely to satisfy a user who wished to consult it for advice. The structure of the system is not quite as simple as the original model, though. The following diagram shows the new structure of the various components in our revised model.

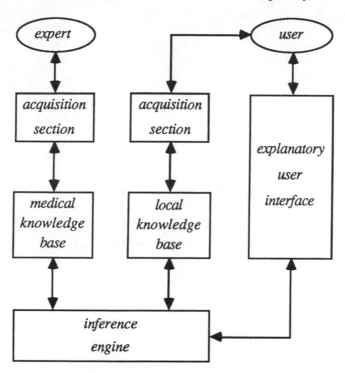

9.2 Expert systems

In revising our diagnosis program so that it takes on some of the characteristics of a medical expert, we have in fact been turning it into an Expert System. Thus the above diagram of the revised model can be viewed as outlining the general structure of an expert system, though some might present it slightly differently. There are differences of opinion about the finer details of what constitutes an expert system. For instance, some prefer to combine both knowledge bases as a single unit, and include the user acquisition section in the user interface. This gives the simpler view of an expert system illustrated on the next page, although it does not give as much information.

Compared with the rather simple structure of an expert system which was given right back in Chapter 1, both these structures seem rather more complicated. So what has happened? To give us the simpler of the two models depicted above, all we have added are components to handle the user interface; and since there are essentially two users (one of which is the expert), there are two user interface components: the *explanatory user interface*, and the *acquisition section*. To obtain the more complex model shown above, we merely separated out the two categories of knowledge: 'permanent' knowledge of the subject, and 'temporary' knowledge for a specific instance of the problem.

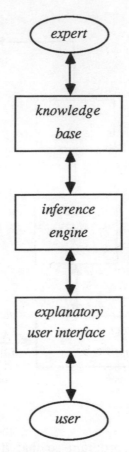

Simplified model of an expert system

Despite the differences in the way people have analysed the structure of expert systems, though, there are certain distinctive characteristics which a system ought to have before it can truly be said to be a full expert system:

(i) The knowledge of the subject area and the reasoning mechanism should be clearly separated in the structure of the system. Put another way, the knowledge base and the inference engine should be distinct and separate sections of the program.

(ii) The system should be able to deal with uncertainty, rather than only clear-cut facts and information.

(iii) The system should be able to explain its train of reasoning in an understandable way.

(iv) The system will generally be limited to a particular, specialised problem area.

(v) The system should be able to acquire more knowledge during its lifetime, by having its knowledge base updated.

Always beware when someone tries to pass off a program as an expert system when it does not have these characteristics. This list of features is not chosen arbitrarily: it has been built up from experience, sometimes bitter experience. The effect of omitting any of the facilities will usually show up some time later, when people gradually stop using the system and show a preference for someone else's system, or even go back to the good old precomputer system.

9.3   Review of the legal adviser program

Now that we have some idea of what to expect of an expert system, let us take another backwards glance, this time at the Prolog formulation of the British Nationality Act. It was suggested at the time that this Prolog program could act as a personal legal adviser or consultant. So how would it stand up as an expert system?

Let us first check its characteristics against the list given in the previous section. There were five features to look for:

(i) *Are the knowledge base and inference engine separated?*

Yes. The Prolog rules representing the Act (which is most of the program) is the knowledge base. The inference engine is just the Prolog system itself which works behind the scenes. We do not actually have to write this bit, but it is there nonetheless.

(ii) *Does it handle uncertainty?*

No. But this is hardly the program's fault: there is not *meant* to be any uncertainty in applying this particular Act, so an ability to handle uncertainty is not required of an Adviser on the British Nationality Act. This implies that it does not take a proper expert to interpret the Act: a methodical moron with a flair for legal language would do. Experts are really only required when judgements have to be made on matters which are less precise, such as 'of good character'. If phrases like this appeared in the legal knowledge base, then there would be uncertainty associated with estimating to what degree the said person's character qualified as 'good'. This could perhaps be accommodated using the probabilities and weights we are familiar with.

(iii) *Does it have an explanation facility?*

No.

(iv) *Is it limited to a specialised problem area?*

Yes. In fact, not only is it limited to the general area of law: it is limited to one particular Act. This would be like having a legal specialist whose speciality was the British Nationality Act.

(v) *Can it acquire more knowledge during its lifetime?*

It should not have to, unless amendments to the Act are subsequently made. If this happens, the corresponding Prolog clauses can be edited by hand, just as any other Prolog program would be modified. This is rather awkward.

Thus, the system does not qualify as an expert system. This is partly because the problem does not really require an expert system in the proper sense. Perhaps the main shortcoming of the program is the lack of an explanation facility. However, if the Prolog approach was applied to a wider range of laws and Acts which did include some uncertainty, then an expert system would definitely be required. Whether it could be trusted is a matter of hot debate, as we have already seen!

The Prolog version of the British Nationality Act was in fact developed by the Imperial team as something closer to an expert system than our description might suggest. Their version provides an explanation facility, and the user is queried for specific information as and when required. The following is based on a small extract from an actual session, where the user is trying to determine whether or not Fred is a British citizen. Anything which is entered by the user is in bold type. We have also added comments (in curly brackets) to explain the system's behaviour and responses.

{ *The user asks the question in the following format:* }

Is fred a British citizen on date(1,may,1986) by section S?

{ *As the system now follows its rules defining citizenship, it discovers it needs certain information about Fred. It therefore will query the user. These queries are generated by the 'user acquisition section', and the information supplied is added to the user knowledge base* }

When was fred was born? **date(29,june,1982)**
Is it true that fred died before date(1,may,1986)? **no**
Is it true that fred was born in the uk? **yes**
Who is the father of fred? **why**

{ *Note that instead of answering this last question, the user has requested to know why the system wants to know this. The special reply* 'why' *activates the explanatory interface, which will now give an explanation of what the system could infer if it had this information:* }

{ *First, why it wants to know the father of Fred:*}

```
if    X is the father of fred
then X is a parent of fred
```

{ *Now, why it wants to know if X is a parent of Fred:*}

```
if    X is a parent of fred
and   X is a British citizen on
      date(29,june,1982)
then fred has a parent who qualifies under
      section_1_1 on date(29,june,1982)
```

{ *Why it wants to know if Fred has a parent who qualifies under section 1.-(1) on 29th June 1982:* }

```
fred was born in the uk
fred was born on date(29,june,1982)
date(29,june,1982) is after or on
commencement, so
if    fred has a parent who qualifies under
      section_1_1 on date(29,june,1982)
then fred acquires British citizenship
      on date(29,june,1982) by section_1_1
```

{ *Finally, why it wants to know this last point:* }

```
fred is alive on date(1,may,1986), so
if    fred acquires British citizenship
      on date(29,june,1982) by section_1_1
and date(1,may,1986) is after or on
                    date(29,june,1982)
and not [fred ceases to be a British citizen
            on date Y
            and Y is between
                date(29,january,1982) and
                date(1,may,1986)]
then fred is a British citizen on
      date(1,may,1986) by section_1_1
```

{ *The system now tries again to get its question answered:* }

```
Who is the father of fred?
```

This explanation is produced automatically, and obviously takes a bit of getting used to before it is much use.

9.4   Expert system shells

Suppose that the manager of a car maintenance firm has an acute shortage of trainee car mechanics, and has a queue of irate customers needing faults in their cars diagnosed and repaired. The manager contacts you to see if you could produce a computerised fault-finding system which would help in any way possible. It is needed in days rather than months, and money is no obstacle. This obviously requires a system which is rather like an expert system.

Let us go back to our medical diagnosis program. It should be clear that it has no understanding of the illnesses or symptoms it processes; it does not realise how uncomfortable it is to have influenza, or the inconvenience of a runny nose. The details in the knowledge base are just facts and figures which, for all it knows, could be about anything, not necessarily people. The system will still work, for instance, if we change the names of the illnesses and the symptoms, and play around a bit with the probabilities. The results may not mean anything, but this is not the concern of the system. For instance, it would quite happily accept and operate with symptom names like:

```
car_wont_start
petrol_gauge_low
```

and illness names such as:

```
flat_battery
dirty_spark_plugs
```

In fact, if we whip out the medical knowledge base, and replace it with a knowledge base in the same format about the illnesses which cars have, and the symptoms which faulty (or *ill*) cars display, then the rest of the system will continue to operate quite merrily. This would straightaway give us a system which diagnoses faults in cars, and outputs the most likely causes of particular malfunctions. For instance, a diagnosis query:

```
?-illness (Fault, Probability).
```

might typically produce the response:

```
Fault = flat_battery
Probability = 62;
Fault = out_of_petrol
Probability = 18;
no
```

We could now use this system as something of an adviser in the mechanics of cars. Admittedly the treatment which has to be applied in the light of the system's diagnosis will differ for mechanical patients from that for human patients. But the diagnosis process itself is the same.

As an example of some of the entries which might be included in the new knowledge base, the following clauses give information on the illnesses out_of_petrol and dirty_spark_plugs:

```
illness (no_petrol, 1,
        [symptom(petrol_gauge_low, 100, 1),
         symptom(car_wont_start, 90, 2)]).

illness (dirty_spark_plugs, 5,
        [symptom(car_serviced_recently, 1, 50),
         symptom(car_wont_start, 90, 8)]).
```

If this information is interpreted in the same way that the medical knowledge base was, then we can deduce from these two clauses, for instance, that:

- On average, one car in a hundred (1%) which requires the attentions of a mechanic has run out of petrol.
- The petrol gauge of a car with no petrol will always be low.
- Of all the cars with low petrol gauges, we would expect to find one in a hundred which have not actually run out of petrol. The gauge could be low because of a blown fuse.
- One in twenty (5%) cars which require attention have dirty spark plugs.
- Nine out of ten (90%) cars with dirty spark plugs will not start.
- Eight per cent of cars which will not start do not have dirty spark plugs.

Note: These actual figures are highly unreliable, and we would have to consult an expert car mechanic to estimate the various probabilities more accurately. This is actually the major part of constructing an expert system, and can be far from easy. It is not really a programming task, since the knowledge is easy enough to represent once an expert has given the probabilities.

Thus, we have outlined how to develop a computerised system which helps to diagnose car faults, and it was not difficult. Note how it was achieved — by taking an existing expert system, 'scooping out' the old knowledge base, and inserting new knowledge about the new problem area. The rest of the system, including the inference engine, stayed the same. It would not be very difficult to carry out this process again. Suppose the next plea for assistance came to us, not from a car mechanic, but from a farmer who was having trouble with some crops, which were being attacked by various nasty fungi. We could repeat the process: scoop out all the previous knowledge, leaving a 'hollow' expert system; then add a new knowledge base giving details of plant diseases caused by fungi, and their symptoms. Without changing anything else, we would have a new expert system.

Clearly, if we were in the business of building expert systems for a range of customers, a most important starting point would be this idea of a 'hollow' expert system — one with all the required features of a first-rate expert system, except no actual knowledge. It would be worthwhile investing effort in a good user interface, with a proper explanation facility and good knowledge acquisition facilities, since these components could all be reused. This hollow *shell* of an expert system is called, not surprisingly, an *Expert System Shell*. Several of these shells are available commercially; they tend to differ in the user interface and in the way the inference engine does its reasoning. To build an expert system for a particular application, only the knowledge base has to be added (using the knowledge acquisition section which is supplied as part of the shell). Although we say 'only', this can still be a major task. Extracting an expert's knowledge in the expert's own subject can be tricky, since often an expert is not actually consciously aware of how he or she uses this knowledge. This task of knowledge extraction is impressively called *knowledge elicitation*. It usually has to be carried out by someone trained in the skills of extracting knowledge from experts. Such people nowadays operate under the job description of *knowledge engineers*.

10

Epilog

If you have ever climbed a mountain, you will know the feeling of thinking you have almost made it to the top, and pausing to survey the ground covered so far. With a well-earned feeling of satisfaction you prepare for the final assault, only to discover yet another peak beyond what you thought was the top. Ideally, this realisation should not be discouraging, but should produce a renewed determination to tackle what lies in front.

In many ways, we have reached just such a point in our consideration of Prolog and its applications. We have certainly come a long way from those early steps of Chapters 1 and 2. A reader should now be in a position to tackle quite a wide range of everyday programming applications, and should be able to construct very useful Prolog programs which solve real-life problems. This is no mean achievement in itself. In addition, two major themes in the application of Prolog have been explored in Part 2. The first of these is language translation. This topic would normally be regarded as considerably beyond the scope of a book of this nature. But with the help of a suitable notation in the form of Prolog, the problem has proved manageable. The second theme has been that of Expert Systems. This is a new subject, and often regarded with awe by those who have not come to an understanding of the principles and terminology associated with expert systems. Yet, by considering two graded preparatory case studies, the fundamental requirements and structure of an expert system have turned out to be not as complex as their reputation sometimes suggests. So as we look backwards and survey the ground already covered, perhaps a feeling of satisfaction at this point is not totally unwarranted.

The tendency at this point, though, is to think that we have almost made it: to think that there is not much more to programming in Prolog, and that the techniques described in this book to date will be sufficient for all that lies ahead. In actual fact, there are several problems still to be encountered and overcome. These are important issues which often become apparent only when addressing large problems and when writing large Prolog programs. These have studiously been avoided to date; this is not to give the impression that there are no problems for a Prolog programmer, but has been done for at least two reasons:

(i) A reader with limited time to devote to learning Prolog, and who may be undertaking only a short course in the subject, will obviously want to learn those aspects of the language which will be the most useful and the most productive. This book has intentionally selected those features of Prolog which come into this category, and has omitted detailed description of less essential features of Prolog which can cause confusion.

(ii) Some of the omitted features of Prolog actually go against the true spirit of Prolog. In many cases, they are there to improve the performance of a program which already works. There is a danger that, if these aspects are discussed in depth while learning the core of the language, then the underlying philosophy of Prolog may become obscured.

So this book has deliberately not covered every aspect of Prolog. Nevertheless, this final chapter is included to let the reader know of some of the peaks still to be conquered, and some of the problems ahead for the serious programmer. The chapter also aims to prepare the reader for these problems, but is not intended to provide the solutions.

The remainder of this chapter discusses three problems which can arise in putting the lessons of this book into practice. We do not really give solutions to these problems: that would require another volume. But, where appropriate, mention is made of the current thinking about where solutions to these problems lie. The reader is also directed to some further reading which may prove helpful in investigating the subject more thoroughly. The three problems which are considered are:

- Can we improve the speed of Prolog programs?
- Can anything be done with a program which gets too large for the computer's memory?
- Why are expert systems not in more widespread use?

10.1   Improving the speed of Prolog programs

It can be rather perplexing to write a Prolog predicate which is logically correct, only to find that the system takes several seconds (or even longer) to answer a query. However, with a more in-depth understanding of *how* Prolog finds solutions, a programmer can improve the speed with which a goal either succeeds or fails.

Recall that Prolog's method of evaluating a goal is in effect to carry out a methodical and relentless *search* for solutions. This may involve investigating several avenues which eventually prove unfruitful. Indeed, before a goal can be shown to fail, *all* possible paths to a solution need to be tried. It is this which often causes the system's performance to appear very slow. If the system could cut out a lot of the redundant searching, and be prevented from searching unfruitful paths, then performance could obviously be improved.

Prolog does indeed provide a mechanism whereby the programmer can direct the system to cut out some of this redundant searching. This mechanism is called the *cut*, which is a built-in predicate. It effectively says to the system: 'carry on from this cut, but do not backtrack past this point'. The cut is used by the programmer when a point is reached where the programmer knows there are no new solutions which could be found by backtracking.

The cut is a rather difficult concept to understand and to use safely. Its use and operation are major subjects in themselves, and beyond the scope of this book. However, if the reader needs to improve the performance of a program, then there are some other books which treat issues like the cut in more depth. Some do this more successfully than others, but the reader may wish to consult the following:

- Clocksin, W.F. and Mellish, C.S. (1987) *Programming in Prolog*, 3rd edn, Springer Verlag, Berlin.
- Malpas, J. (1987) *Prolog: a relational language and its applications*, Prentice-Hall International, Inc., Englewood Cliffs, N.J.
- Bratko, I. (1986) *Prolog Programming for Artificial Intelligence*, Addison-Wesley, Reading, Ma.

10.2   Space limitations

The example databases and knowledge bases given throughout this book should have no difficulty in fitting into the memory of a computer. To have enlarged the examples would only have added to the length, and not the understanding. However, in some cases, a real-life database would be a different matter. For instance, in the simple library catalogue program in Chapter 4, a typical catalogue could in practice have several thousand entries. The internal memory of the computer would very quickly become full, leaving no room for the rest of the database.

To overcome the limitations of a restricted memory capacity, computers usually have some form of *backing store*, such as floppy disks or a hard disk. If a complete Prolog program cannot fit into internal memory, then parts of it must be held on backing store. If one of these parts is required for answering a query, it must first be copied from backing store into internal memory.

Virtual memory

Some less sophisticated Prolog systems which permit a program to be split across internal memory and backing store require careful use by the programmer. The programmer has to state within the program when a predicate's definition should be copied from backing store into internal memory. The program may also have to delete a resident predicate to make room for the new one.

Thankfully, some more recent Prolog systems will handle the management of backing store automatically. When a predicate is required, the system will first look to see if it is already in internal memory. If not, the predicate will be loaded from backing store. In doing this, the system will also make room, if necessary, by choosing another resident predicate for deletion. This is all done automatically, and means that the use of backing store is invisible to the programmer. The only difference from having a bigger internal memory is that the program will execute more slowly. Since this facility gives the impression of a much larger memory capacity, it is referred to as a *virtual memory* facility. When choosing between different versions of Prolog, the presence or absence of a virtual memory facility is a significant factor.

10.3   Problems with Expert Systems

Many applications which are candidates for computerisation require programs which come into the category of expert systems. Customers are also prepared to pay well for such systems. So given such an attractive market, it is strange that expert systems are not in as widespread use as we might have expected. Two reasons for this state of affairs have gradually become apparent, and a third is emerging. The first has to do with extracting the knowledge base from an expert (called *knowledge elicitation*). The second has to do with managing and structuring a large knowledge base. Finally, there is the problem of legal responsibility. There are no easy answers to these problems as yet, and researchers are still only at the early stages of tackling them.

Knowledge elicitation

It has been discovered that the process of extracting knowledge from an expert, and expressing it in rule form, is an extremely slow one. It can take months, maybe even longer, to build up a viable knowledge base. If the expert system is for use in a developing technological application, then a particularly unfortunate situation arises: the knowledge base becomes out of date before the system is ready! This obviously undermines the whole operation of the system.

This has become a real problem, and the process of knowledge elicitation is now the subject of considerable research. One approach which is favoured by some is to develop better ways of representing knowledge. Prolog's way of representing knowledge using simple rules was certainly an advance over what was available at the time. But it is not necessarily ideal. Work is in progress to develop more powerful versions of Prolog, which will include ideas from mathematics and from formal logic.

Knowledge management

One feature of an expert system is that its knowledge base is continually updated as a result of the ongoing process of knowledge elicitation. The knowledge base thus grows in size, but this growth is undisciplined, unplanned and without structure. The result is that a large knowledge base can become an unstructured, homogeneous mass of rules which is eventually unmanageable. At least one well-known commercial expert system, which has been used as a model and as a symbol of the success of expert systems, has recently come to grief over this issue.

Bringing order out of a disorganised and unstructured mass of information is one of the most intelligent and creative activities which humans perform. Whether it be in office administration, in government, in science, in literature, or whatever, a mark of intelligence is the ability to classify, analyse and structure information, and then to reorganise affairs so that order is imposed and things are simplified. If expert systems are to have a significant lifetime, and keep their knowledge base up to date without collapsing in a disorganised heap, then they will have to be given some ability to organise and structure their knowledge base automatically. This is an extremely difficult problem, and a suitable solution is still a long way off. But again, it has of necessity become the subject of considerable research.

Legal responsibility

A human expert or consultant can occasionally give advice which is negligent or incompetent. If this wrong advice can be shown to lead to an accident, then the expert can be held responsible and sued for damages. This is an accepted risk of acting as an expert. But if instead of a human expert we use a computerised expert — an expert system — then who is responsible? Can a computer program be sued? Or should the suppliers of the system be held responsible? If the latter is the case, then the situation is very worrying for anyone constructing an expert system. The implications of this state of affairs were discussed earlier in Chapter 8, when considering the use in practice of our medical diagnosis program. It could mean that no-one would be prepared to supply an expert system if they were legally liable for its operation. It is also unlikely that an insurance firm would insure it. Perhaps the only reasonable option is to hold responsible the person who relies and acts upon the advice which the expert system gives. This would mean that a user would be much more cautious about acting upon the advice of an expert system, and the role of expert systems would become significantly lower key than expected. Since someone would need to be an expert to know whether or not the advice of the expert system is dependable, it makes one wonder about the point of having an expert system in the first place! It could well be that these legal aspects of accountability will ultimately prove to be the greatest restricting factor on the uptake of expert system technology, rather than the technical problems in actually constructing an expert system.

For some further reading on the whole subject of Expert Systems, there is some material in the following books which may prove helpful:

- Forsyth, R. ed. (1984) *Expert Systems: Principles and case studies*, Chapman and Hall, London.
- Jackson, P. (1986) *Introduction to Expert Systems*, Addison-Wesley, Reading, Ma.
- Hayes-Roth, F., Waterman, D.A. and Lenat, D.B. eds. (1983) *Building Expert Systems*, Addison-Wesley, Reading, Ma.

Solutions

One of the purposes of the exercises included in the first part of this book is for use as assessed practical assignments for coursework. The reader will therefore understand why solutions to all the exercises are not given! Instead, solutions are included for one exercise from each chapter.

CHAPTER 2

2 A family tree

```
male (philip).
female (elizabeth).
male (charles).
female (anne).
male (andrew).
male (edward).
female (diana).
male (mark).
female (sarah).
male (william).
male (harry).
male (peter).
female (zara).

married_to (philip, elizabeth).
married_to (elizabeth, philip).
married_to (charles, diana).
married_to (diana, charles).
married_to (mark, anne).
married_to (anne, mark).
```

```
married_to (andrew, sarah).
married_to (sarah, andrew).

child_of (charles, philip).
child_of (charles, elizabeth).
child_of (anne, philip).
child_of (anne, elizabeth).
child_of (andrew, philip).
child_of (andrew, elizabeth).
child_of (edward, philip).
child_of (edward, elizabeth).
child_of (william, charles).
child_of (william, diana).
child_of (harry, charles).
child_of (harry, diana).
child_of (peter, mark).
child_of (peter, anne).
child_of (zara, mark).
child_of (zara, anne).
```

(i)   ?-child_of (Child, anne).

(ii)   ?-child_of (william, Parent).

(iii)   ?-child_of (edward, Parent1),
           child_of (edward, Parent2),
           not (Parent1 = Parent2),
           child_of (Brother, Parent1),
           child_of (Brother, Parent2),
           not (Brother = edward),
           male (Brother).

(iv)   ?-child_of (peter, Parent),
           child_of (Parent, Grandparent).

CHAPTER 3

3 Management structures

The various positions in the illustrated management structure will be
represented by the following Prolog objects:

```
director
finance_manager
administration_manager
```

```
production_manager
finance_officer
clerk
cashier
receptionist
typist
telephonist
sales_officer
stores_manager
publicity_officer
```

The direct working relationships are defined by the following rules:

```
works_for (finance_manager, director).
works_for (administration_manager, director).
works_for (production_manager, director).
works_for (finance_officer, finance_manager).
works_for (clerk, finance_officer).
works_for (cashier, finance_officer).
works_for (receptionist,
           administration_manager).
works_for (typist, administration_manager).
works_for (telephonist,
           administration_manager).
works_for (sales_officer, production_manager).
works_for (stores_manager,production_manager).
works_for (publicity_officer,
           production_manager).
```

The additional predicates are as follows:

(i)   boss_of (X, Y) :- works_for (Y, X).

(ii)   under (X, Y) :- works_for (X, Y).

        under (X, Y) :- works_for (X, Z),
                        under (Z, Y).

(iii)   over (X, Y) :- under (Y, X).

CHAPTER 4

3 More list operations

Deleting from a list

```
delete ([], _, []).

delete ([Element|Tail], Element, List_out) :-
    delete (Tail, Element, List_out).

delete ([Head|Tail], Element, [Head|Rest]) :-
    not (Head = Element),
    delete (Tail, Element, Rest).
```

The second rule covers the case where the first item in the list is the one which is being deleted; in this case, we still have to continue deleting any further occurrences from the rest of the list.

Appending two lists

The approach is to work through the first of the two lists to be combined, element by element. If the first list is empty, it is easy to append the second list: the result *is* the second list. If the first list is not empty, then the head of this list will be the head of the combined list; the tail of the combined list is then found by appending the second list to the tail of the first list. This gives the following definition of append:

```
append ([], L, L).

append ([Head| Tail], List2, [Head| Rest]) :-
    append (Tail, List2, Rest).
```

CHAPTER 5

2 Formatting list output

The list to be written will as usual be processed one element at a time, by a recursive predicate. Since in general the next element to be displayed will not be displayed at the start of a line, it is necessary to know how many items have so far been displayed on the current line. If Width items have already been displayed on this line, then a new line should be taken. Most of the work is done by a separate predicate:

```
format_rest (List, Width, number of items displayed so
                                far on this line)
```

So at the very start, we can define `format_list` by:

```
format_list (List, Width) :-
     format_rest (List, Width, 0),
     nl.
```

where `format_rest` is defined as follows:

```
format_rest ([], _, _).
```

```
format_rest (List, Width, Width) :-
     nl,
     format_rest (List, Width, 0).
```

```
format_rest ([Head| Tail], Width, N_so_far) :-
     write (Head),
     write (' '),
     N_plus1 is N_so_far + 1,
     format_rest (Tail, Width, N_plus1).
```

Index